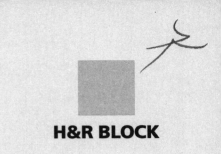

H&R BLOCK

just plain smart ™

home
buying
advisor

This book is available for special discounts for bulk purchases for sales promotions or premiums. Special editions, including personalized covers, excerpts of existing books, and corporate imprints, can be created in large quantities for special needs. For more information, write to Special Markets/ Premium Sales, 1745 Broadway, MD 6-2, New York, NY, 10019 or e-mail specialmarkets@randomhouse.com.

Random House is a registered trademark of Random House, Inc.

Please address inquiries about electronic licensing of reference products, for use on a network or in software or on CD-ROM, to the Subsidiary Rights Department, Random House Reference, fax 212-572-6003.

Visit the Random House Reference Web site: www.randomhouse.com

Typeset and printed in the United States of America.

Library of Congress Cataloging-in-Publication Data is available.

Edition

0 9 8 7 6 5 4 3 2 1
2004
0-375-72021-9

H&R BLOCK

just plain smart™

home
buying
advisor

find the right home in the right neighborhood at the right price

ask the right questions of your real estate agent, lender, and home inspector

understand the essentials of mortgages, closings, and insurance

avoid common mistakes that home buyers make

**RANDOM HOUSE
REFERENCE
NEW YORK**

table of contents with selected topics

Introduction

For most of us, buying a home is a big deal. If you are like most people, you will only buy one or two homes in your lifetime. Whether you are dreaming about finding and purchasing your first home, or if you already own a home and are thinking about your next home, you have many decisions to make. Between searching for the right real estate agent and searching for the perfect home in a neighborhood that is right for you, to making an offer and applying for a mortgage, the process can be complicated. In fact, it can be a little overwhelming.

Understanding the ins and outs of the home buying process can take some time and effort. If you want to exercise more control over the process and help assure a successful outcome for yourself, you need to understand how the process works. Once you understand the steps involved, you will be able to take advantage of opportunities as they present themselves and avoid pitfalls along the way.

The **H&R Block Home Buying Advisor,** one of several personal planning guides in the H&R Block just plain smart™ Advisor Series, will help you make informed decisions and avoid major stumbling blocks as you go through the steps of finding a home, financing it, closing the deal, and enjoying home ownership. Because taxes play a big role in home buying and home ownership, H&R Block, the world's largest tax services company, has the experience to understand your goals and the expertise to help you achieve them. Use the H&R Block just plain smart™ Advisor Series to put our experience to work for you.

How to Use This Book

The **Home Buying Advisor** is designed to help you gain control over the home-buying process. It covers a wide variety of topics, from helping you understand the difference between your wants and needs, working with a real estate agent, guiding you through the details of financing and negotiating, and revealing how you can maintain and unlock hidden value in your home. The book features dozens of worksheets and sidebars that cover useful "fast facts," action-packed "smart steps," and clear "plain talk" definitions. It also contains scenarios derived from real-life situations.

We have organized the **Home Buying Advisor** as a step-by-step resource with helpful tools to guide you through the home buying process. Keep it handy and consult it throughout the process as certain events occur, such as getting a home inspected or purchasing insurance. The book will help you make more informed decisions along the way.

Online Learning Resources

Make the most of your **Home Buying Advisor.** Throughout the book, you'll find numerous online smart steps that will enable you to immediately put into practice (via the Internet) some of the topics that have just been covered in the book. You will gain access to a variety of interactive tools and calculators that will help you achieve your home ownership goals.

Look for the Web site address hrblock.com/advisor inside the smart steps (pictured at right), log on, and get started today!

What's the Next Step?

Decide how much of the **Home Buying Advisor** applies to your personal situation and determine what steps you need to take. Turn to the **Home Buying Advisor** whenever you make or modify plans. It will help you ask informed ques-

smart step

Start Now!

Use online learning resources to get started today.

Log on to
hrblock.com/advisor

tions of real estate agents, lenders, inspectors, sellers, and others you will encounter along the way. Whether you do it all on your own or work with the other professionals, you will be better equipped to handle your home buying options wisely.

Acknowledgments

While it is not possible to list everyone who made the **H&R Block Home Buying Advisor** possible, we would like to acknowledge the following organizations and individuals for their many contributions to this book: **Random House Reference** ▦ **and the many dedicated associates and tax and financial professionals of H&R Block.**

H&R Block

HOME OWNERSHIP 101:

An Introduction to Home Ownership

"A house is made of walls and beams; a home is built with love and dreams."

—Author Unknown

Congratulations! If you are reading this book, you have decided to investigate the opportunities associated with buying a home. The decision to buy a home, to pursue a part of the American Dream, can be one of the most financially and emotionally rewarding experiences in your life. But buying a home is a major life decision and involves a process that can reward those who plan ahead and penalize those who don't. This book will both help inform you about and help you plan each step of the home buying process.

Buying a home is time consuming, but it is a process you do not want to rush. Chances are that it is the largest investment you will make in your life. If you accept that there is a lot to learn, and take the time to learn it, you can help yourself make the right decisions along the way.

Home ownership is a basic building block of society. It fosters stability and a sense of community. Therefore, government policies and tax laws, both local and federal, foster home ownership. How do they do that, what does it mean for you, and why is home ownership so important? Read on.

Owning versus Renting

Many people assume, and rightly so, that owning a home is better than renting one. Certainly the chance to build **equity** in a property you own makes home ownership attractive, but when the garbage disposal needs to be repaired or replaced, or the roof starts leaking, it is nice to have a landlord to call. So the first thing to realize is that home ownership is substantially different from renting.

RENTING VERSUS OWNING	
RENTING	**OWNING**
Fixed costs: Your rent is your rent, and you know exactly what you will pay each month.	Variable costs: You must pay for upkeep, and adjustable rate loans can fluctuate.
You never earn any equity.	Your equity in the home grows as you make payments and through potential **appreciation**.
Renting a home is not an investment, only a place to live.	Home ownership can be a good investment as well as a place to live.
No long-term commitment: You are only obligated for the term of the lease. If your personal situation (such as financial or employment) or general economic conditions (such as mass unemployment) change, you don't own something that may actually decline in value.	Long-term commitment required: Even if your personal situation (such as financial or employment) changes, you are still obligated to pay for the home until you can sell it.
Renting a home requires little upkeep.	Home ownership requires ongoing upkeep and maintenance.
Few costs are required for you to be able to move in.	A substantial down payment and significant fees are normally required to purchase a home.
You are not in charge and there is little chance to make it your own.	You are the king or queen of your castle. You can remodel and make as many changes as you like and your budget allows.
There are no federal tax advantages to renting.	There are definite tax advantages to owning.

plain talk

The increase in value of an asset is known as appreciation.

Even with all the advantages of home ownership, not everyone is ready to buy a home. If you answer *yes* to the following questions, you may be ready to consider buying a home.

- **Do you plan to live in the same area for several more years?** If you expect to move to another area within the next few years, renting may be a better option. It could cost you more to buy and sell the home than the benefits you would gain from ownership.

- **Do you have a steady income that will enable you to make mortgage payments for the next fifteen to thirty years?** If you don't expect a reliable source of income for the foreseeable future, you may not be ready for a home.
- **Do you have the time and money to maintain a home?** Keeping the grass mowed, the hedges trimmed, the roof from leaking, the toilets working, and the dozens of other odd jobs that go with home ownership can take a toll on your time and pocketbook. Owning a home is a big commitment.
- **Do you have the money to cover the down payment?** The amount required for a down payment depends on the lender. Some lenders require a down payment as low as 3 percent of the home's purchase price, and in some cases no down payment may be required. Be sure to consider the amount you will need for closing costs, such as points and other fees. Also keep in mind that if your down payment is less than 20 percent of the home's price, you may have to pay **private mortgage insurance** (PMI) each month.
- **Do you have a credit rating solid enough to qualify for a mortgage?** If you're unsure about your credit history, review your credit report and do whatever is necessary to bring your credit rating up to par.

If you answered *yes* to all five questions, then you're probably ready to consider buying a home. The sooner you buy, the sooner you can start enjoying the advantages of home ownership.

Home Ownership Makes Financial Sense

Buying a home can be one of the smartest financial decisions you will make. One reason is that home ownership carries less risk than many other investments. Other investments are subject to a host of outside factors that affect the value of the investment. Stocks can rise or fall for a variety of reasons including rumors, gossip, or war. Bonds can rise or fall the day a new inflation report hits. Real estate, while certainly subject to market fluctuations,

plain talk

Private mortgage insurance (PMI) is insurance coverage that protects the lender if the buyer defaults on the loan.

is not so whimsical, so it does not generally greatly appreciate or depreciate in a day.

Buying your own home can be a great opportunity to grow financially. Home ownership tends to be a solid investment and usually yields good returns. Many of the richest people in the country, people such as Donald Trump and Merv Griffin, owe a portion of their fortunes to real estate.

The Beauty of Leverage

Besides stability, pride of ownership, equity growth, and a potential gain when you sell your home, home ownership has the added advantage over other investments of a system that allows buyers to use a little of their own money and a lot of other people's money. That's called leverage. Leverage is one of the most important reasons why buying a home is one of the best financial decisions you can make.

Most investments require that you put up all the money needed to purchase them. Take the stock market, for example. Unless you are buying on **margin** (which most of us don't), you are required to pay for the shares you purchase. There is no one else's money to use but your own. This is true for other investments as well, including bonds, mutual funds, bank deposits, coins, stamps, and art. If you want to own it, you generally have to pay for it all up front. That is true everywhere in the world of investments, except real estate.

In real estate, you can put down as little as 3–5 percent of the money necessary to purchase a home. Rarely are you expected to put down more than 20 percent. The mortgage lender (or sometimes the seller) loans you the rest of the money to buy the property. You are using other people's money to buy a valuable asset.

plain talk

Buying a stock on margin means that you borrow the money for the investment from your broker and use that money to purchase stock.

smart step

Start Now!

Calculate the financial value of owning a home versus renting.

Log on to
hrblock.com/advisor

The advantages of using leverage are twofold. First, leverage significantly increases how much home you can buy. Second, leverage can allow you to eventually make a much bigger gain (assuming your home appreciates, of course) when the time comes to sell your property. You can use a little money to buy a lot of home and as you make your monthly payments, and if your home appreciates, your equity will grow. The more equity you have in your home, the larger your eventual gain may be. You could think of your home as an automatic savings plan.

For example, with $7,500, you could buy $7,500 worth of stocks or bonds or mutual funds or gold. However, let's say that you decided to use your $7,500 to buy a home. Your $7,500 is 5 percent of a $150,000, single-family residence. As such, using leverage, you could use $7,500 of your own money and get a mortgage lender to put down the other $142,500. You would then end up owning an asset worth $150,000. That's leverage, and, yes, it is remarkable.

Mortgage lenders are not the only people who help you buy property using leverage. Sellers sometimes finance part of the mortgage (called "carrying the paper") to help you get into a home as well. As such, it is even possible to buy a home without putting any of your own money down. (For more information, see Chapter 6.) Much more common, however, is getting mortgage lenders and sellers to finance 80–90 percent of the property. That is the rule, not the exception, in real estate.

Leverage can certainly help you to purchase your home using other people's money, but remember you still have to pay for the amount of the loan and the interest, which can add up. In our earlier example of purchasing a $150,000 home with 5 percent down, the loan amount would be $142,500. If you secured a loan at 7 percent for thirty years, you would end up paying about $198,800 in interest, plus the principal amount of $142,500, over the lifetime of the loan. Is it still such a good deal to buy a home with leverage? While it sounds like a lot of money (and it is), you still need to consider any potential appreciation in the value of the home, potential tax benefits you may receive from home ownership, and the fact that you have to live somewhere and will probably have to pay to do so. Leverage just helps make it possible.

Taxes and Your Home

If you buy a home, not only will you get the joy of home ownership, but you may also be able to enjoy reducing your tax liability by deducting home-ownership-related expenses such as points, mortgage loan interest, and real estate taxes. Here are the basic tax-saving elements of home ownership:

Interest—When you pay interest on a qualified home mortgage, you may generally deduct the interest in full as an itemized deduction. The mortgage must be secured by your principal residence or a second residence. For income tax purposes, a principal residence is the one where you live and return to after short absences. You can have only one principal residence at a time. A second residence is one that is for personal purposes only, or, if rented, used for personal purposes for more than the greater of fourteen days or 10 percent of the number of days you rent the home at fair rental value. If you own more than two homes, you may claim the interest deduction on only one as a second residence for any given year. Late payment penalties and **prepayment penalties** are also deductible if such payments are not for a specific service performed in connection with your mortgage loan.

Points—The points you pay are deductible in full in the year paid as an itemized deduction if certain conditions are met. To qualify, the loan has to be for the purchase or improvement of, and be secured by, your principal residence. Charging of points must be an established practice in your area, and the amount of points cannot be excessive. The amount must be computed as a per-

plain talk

Prepayment penalties are fees that some lenders charge when a borrower pays a mortgage (during a specified period after closing) before it is due.

THE CHALLENGE

Mario and Cheryl are a young, married couple who are thinking about starting a family. They dream of owning their own home, but they don't see how they can afford to do so because money is tight. One day, on a whim, they decide to stop by a real estate office, and they meet a real estate agent named Randy. Mario and Cheryl explain to Randy that they have $5,000 in savings and they have no idea how they can get a loan. They do not think they can ever buy the home they want—a three-bedroom home with a two-car garage.

THE PLAN

Although Mario and Cheryl don't have a lot of money, Randy is willing to work with the young couple. They tell him what neighborhood they like, what they think they can afford, and what sort of home they hope to buy. After researching the neighborhood, Randy finds a home that has been on the market for more than a year. He visits the home and speaks with the owner.

Although the house isn't exactly the perfect home for Mario and Cheryl (it has only a one-car garage), the owner of the home is anxious to sell because he has already purchased another home and has been making payments on both homes. Consequently, he is open to considering other options.

Randy comes up with a plan. He suggests that the parties enter into a "lease-option" arrangement whereby Mario and Cheryl lease the home for a year, during which time a part of each month's rent is applied to a down payment if they decide to buy the home at the end of the term. Everyone agrees to this creative plan, which meets the needs of all parties.

After negotiating the terms in the contract, Mario and Cheryl move in, and after a year, the couple decide they want to proceed with buying the home. Following the terms of the contract, the owner held $5,000 of their first year's rent as a down payment toward their purchase of the home. As a bonus, during that same year the couple saved another $2,500. Armed now with $12,500 ($5,000 savings + $5,000 rent payments applied toward purchase + $2,500 additional savings), they secured a loan and bought the home.

centage of the stated principal amount of the mortgage. Finally, the amount you paid at or before closing, plus any points the seller paid, must be at least as much as the points charged. Deducting your points in their entirety in the year of purchase is an option, but it is not required. You can opt to deduct the points over the life of the mortgage. Your tax professional can help you determine which option will be more beneficial to you. If you refinance the mortgage, any points paid must be deducted over the life of the loan.

Real Estate Taxes—If you itemize, you can deduct state, local, and foreign real estate taxes you paid on your home, vacation dwelling, or other real property.

Home Equity Credit Lines—Because mortgage debt is secured by your home, interest on the loan is deductible, subject to certain limitations. You may be able to trade nondeductible debt (such as a large credit card balance or vehicle loan) for debt that is deductible. Although a home equity loan provides tax advantages not available from other loans, never take out a home equity loan unless you are certain you can make the payments. If you fail to repay the loan, one of your most valuable possessions, your home, may be at risk.

By granting you tax deductions for items such as mortgage interest, the government is, in effect, helping make home ownership more affordable. See your tax professional for assistance with the tax consequences of buying and owning a home.

Other Advantages of Home Ownership

Aside from leverage and tax breaks, there are other reasons why home ownership makes financial sense:

Appreciation and Equity Growth—Your financial health improves in two ways when you own a home. First, over time, real estate generally appreciates,

fast fact

The largest private home in the United States is the Biltmore Estate in North Carolina. Completed in 1895, it has 250 rooms, including 35 bedrooms, 43 bathrooms, 3 kitchens, 65 fireplaces, and 1 indoor swimming pool.

which means that the value of your investment should grow. If you sell your home, you should realize a gain. Secondly, as you pay off the loan on the home, your equity in the property grows, too. Between the equity you gain by paying off the loan, and the additional equity you may gain through appreciation, owning your own home can help you build your overall wealth.

Credit—Home ownership, and the ability to pay off a home mortgage in a timely manner, is looked upon very favorably by creditors. You build a strong credit rating by being a homeowner and making your payments on time.

Home ownership, with all its advantages, comes with some concerns as well. Owning a home can be expensive. Even with leverage, coming up with a down payment can be a challenge, as can paying the mortgage every month. If you fail to make the payments, the lender can begin **foreclosure** proceedings to take the home back. Maintenance and upkeep can also take a bite out of your paycheck. And, if something major goes wrong—you lose a job or get divorced, for example—getting out of the home is not always simple.

Understanding the Costs Involved

Once you have decided to buy a home, the question becomes how much home can you afford? This issue is discussed in detail in the next chapter, but suffice it to say at this point that before you do anything, you need to know your price range. To determine your price range, you need to be aware of the various fees and costs associated with buying a home.

The Down Payment—It is possible to buy a home with as little as a 3 percent down payment (using an FHA loan, for example), but it is far more common to put about 10 percent down. If you put 20 percent down, you probably

plain talk

Foreclosure occurs when the owner of real estate fails to make his or her payments and the lender seeks to take title to the home.

won't have to pay private mortgage insurance (PMI) so your monthly payment will be lower.

Monthly Payments—How much can you afford to pay every month? Most lenders consider somewhere between 28 and 32 percent of your gross monthly income a standard and reasonable amount. Remember that the amount you pay will include not just your mortgage payment, but will also generally include taxes and insurance, so plan accordingly.

Lender Fees—Paying points to the lender is not uncommon and it can be one of the fees they charge. One point is equal to 1 percent of the loan amount. Other fees may include loan origination fees, loan application fees, document preparation fees, credit check fees, and appraisal fees.

Impound Fees—Your lender may require you to pay your yearly insurance and estimated taxes into an impound account (sometimes referred to as an escrow or reserve account) each month, or you may want to set it up that way. Here's why: Your yearly property tax payment and insurance bill may be several thousand dollars. It may not be easy to pay these amounts all at one time. An impound account allows you to divide these costs and pay them on a monthly basis.

Other Fees—You may also have to pay title search fees, recording fees, title insurance fees, and inspection fees. These fees (and many others) are explained in more detail later.

We mention these fees not to scare you, but so you understand how expensive it can be to buy a home. It can be a shock to learn that $10,000 of your $40,000 down payment may go to fees, thus reducing the amount of home you can buy. If you are aware of the fees up front, you can make an accurate estimate of how much you can afford to offer on a home.

fast fact

One point equals one percent of your loan. Thus, if you borrow $150,000, one point would be $1,500.

SAMPLE UP-FRONT FEES AND COSTS	
Purchase price:	$150,000
Interest rate:	7 percent
Amount financed:	$142,500

TYPE OF FEE*	COST
Down payment	$ 7,500
Loan origination fee	712
Document preparation	125
Points (1)	1,425
Appraisal	350
Credit report	15
Insurance and tax reserve	610
Inspection	225
Title search	75
Recording fees	25
Total:	**$11,062**

* Sample fees shown for illustration purposes only. Actual fees will vary by lender and location.

How to Proceed and What to Expect

Some people, once they decide it is time to buy a home, do their analysis, decide on a price, jump in, and make an offer within days and after seeing only a few homes. Others methodically analyze every home that comes on the market for months and may see dozens of homes before making an offer. But most people fall somewhere in the middle.

Keep in mind that your home buying process does not happen in a vacuum; the activities of other homebuyers and sellers have an impact on your transactions.

For example, if you decide to buy during a seller's market (when homes are selling quickly and usually for full asking price), beware of the buying frenzy that often accompanies such times. In an active marketplace, homes may be on the market for only a few days or weeks before they are snatched up, so you may not have the luxury of taking your time. By the same token, in a buyer's market (that is, when homes are not selling quickly), you may have all the time you need to get the pick of the litter.

What follows is a description of the home buying process and a rough estimate of how long it might take. Your timeline may be faster or slower. If you need time to save the down payment, the process may take longer than if you are ready to get started now. Set a goal of when you want to move into your home and work backwards from there. You'll want to develop a timetable that is specific to your situation to keep you and the process on track. The items covered will be discussed in more detail throughout the book, but it is helpful to have a bird's-eye view of the overall process.

■ **Four months before moving.** Analyze your financial situation and decide how much home you can afford. Choose the neighborhoods in which you want to look. Find an agent with whom to work. Compare lenders. Get **prequalified or preapproved** for a loan. Begin your home search.

■ **Three months before moving.** Narrow your search. Compare homes. Make a decision. Make an offer. Deal with counteroffers. Negotiate the final contract.

■ **Two months before moving.** Have home inspection completed. Make closing arrangements. Arrange for homeowner's insurance. Deal with potential problems (such as repairs that haven't been finished). Make preliminary moving arrangements.

■ **One month before moving.** Make sure everything is on track. Monitor the lender and escrow company. Arrange for utilities in new home and complete change of address forms.

■ **One week before moving.** Double-check with lender, real estate agent, escrow company, and mover. Make final arrangements. Confirm closing and
signing of all documents.

Understanding where you are headed, however, is only half the battle. The
other thing to understand is how you will get there. It is fairly safe to say that
the process of going from deciding to buy a home to closing the deal will be full
of more twists and turns than you can anticipate. As you go down this winding
path, keep these five rules of the road in mind:

1. **Everything is negotiable**—When we say everything, we mean everything.
   From the price of the home and how much your real estate agent will charge in
   commissions to the terms of the sales contract and mortgage, everything is subject to and open for discussion. Because everything in the home buying process
   is negotiable, you can use this fact to your advantage. When you are presented
   with something you don't like, make a counteroffer. When language in a contract is unsuitable, change it. When a home you like has a broken concrete slab,
   make fixing it a condition of the offer. Everyone involved in the process, including your real estate professional, the lender, and the appraiser, knows that this is
   a fluid process, so you need to be aware of it, too.

2. **Try and create a win-win situation**—The worst deals are those in which a
   stronger party hammers a weaker party into a deal the latter doesn't like. When
   that happens, the weaker party, who got the raw end of the deal, is likely to
   breach the agreement down the road. It is far better to create a deal that everyone can live with.

3. **Be choosy, but be practical**—You may have a dream home in mind, and you
   may find it. Then again, you may not. Part of the fun is finding a home that will
   work for you and then making it your own.

4. **Remember that there is no perfect time to buy**—You may be tempted to
   wait until interest rates go down a bit, or until the market slows down a bit. Your

reasons for waiting may be right, but your guess may also be wrong. Rates and prices could go up instead of down. When you are ready, go for it.

5. **Have fun**—This process will be stressful at times, but it should also be fun. Take it seriously (again, it will probably be the largest purchase of your life), but take pleasure in the process. The chance to pick a home you adore in a neighborhood you love is a rare opportunity, so enjoy the experience.

Did You Know That . . .?

You don't need to know everything about how buying and financing a home works to actually purchase a home. But the more you do know, the better prepared you will be to make informed choices and decisions along the way.

- **The amount of home you can afford depends on a number of factors, only one of which is how much money you have?** See Chapter 2 to determine how much home you can afford and the amount of money you may qualify to borrow.

- **Certain people who weren't even in the military may be eligible for a Veteran's Administration (VA) loan?** See Chapter 3 to learn more about the many different types of loans available and what the benefits are of each type.

- **A Realtor® and a real estate agent may perform similar functions, but the two are not exactly the same?** See Chapter 4 for more information about working with real estate professionals.

- **Your home may end up being a house, a condominium, a town home, or a cooperative?** See Chapter 5 to learn more about your housing options and what to look for in each.

- **Even if you have bad credit, you probably have options for purchasing a home?** See Chapter 6 for information on creative ways to purchase a home.

- **The real estate contract is essential to purchasing a home and can protect your interests?** See Chapter 7 for information on the basics of real estate contracts, what to look for, and what to avoid.

smart step

When looking at the price of homes, keep current market conditions in mind. If a home has been on the market for some time, you might be able to purchase it for up to 10 percent less than the asking price.

- **Not having a home inspected before purchasing it is like playing with fire, and you will most likely get burned?** See Chapter 8 to learn more about home inspections so you are sure you are getting what you paid for.
- **There are numerous issues that can come up in the home buying and financing process that can cause the deal to fall apart, costing you time, money, or your dream home?** See Chapter 9 to learn more about how you can reduce the chances that something will go wrong and what to do in case something does.
- **There are different ways to legally hold title to real estate?** See Chapter 10 to understand more about your options and other important decisions you'll need to make before closing on your new home.
- **Without homeowner's insurance, most of us could probably never get a mortgage or afford to tie up a large portion of our assets in purchasing a home?** See Chapter 11 to understand what to look for when considering options for insuring your home and how insurance can help protect you from financial devastation in the event of a loss.
- **Your home may contain more value than you think?** See Chapter 12 to understand more about unlocking the hidden value in your home through a home equity line of credit and how to maintain the value of your home.

Some people have a great deal of knowledge about home buying. But many of us purchase only one or two homes during our lifetimes, so we need to get it right the first time. Reading the **Home Buying Advisor** will help provide you with the knowledge you need to get started and to be a more informed consumer when working with different professionals in the home buying process.

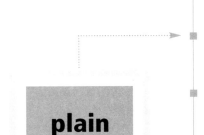

plain talk

A legal interest in (ownership of) real estate is known as title.

the ESSENTIALS

1. Owning your own home involves more responsibility than renting, but it also offers substantial benefits.

2. Equity in your home allows you to get ahead financially. The chance to build equity in your home should be a positive factor in making your home buying decision.

3. Leverage allows you to use other people's money to buy and control an asset (your home) that you otherwise might not be able to afford.

4. Don't underestimate the fees involved when deciding how much home you can afford. They can be substantial.

5. Purchasing a home is a time-consuming but rewarding process. A home is a big investment, so take the time to make sure that everything is done right. Don't rush the process.

fast fact

On average, since 1950 single-family homes have appreciated in value every year.

2 [YOUR HOME BUYING PLAN:

Mapping Out Your Path
to Home Ownership

]

"It takes as much energy to wish as it does to plan."
—Eleanor Roosevelt

smart step

Start Now!

Determine how much home you can afford.

Log on to
hrblock.com/advisor

Buying the right home in the right neighborhood at the right price takes careful planning. You must determine how much money you have to spend, how much home you can afford to buy, where to look, what you want, and who can help you. An inexperienced homebuyer who starts the process without doing his or her homework can be making a big mistake.

Creating a home buying plan helps ensure that you end up where you want to be. Think of it this way: A pilot would never fly from New York to Miami without first coming up with a flight plan. The plan indicates where the plane is going, how much fuel is needed, what route the pilot will take, how long the flight will take, and where the plane will land. Well, that's what your home buying plan is. It is your plan for how you will get to where you want to be from where you currently are. So let's get going!

How Much Home Can You Afford?

The first part of your home buying plan concerns how much home you can afford. A host of decisions depend upon that piece of information, including what neighborhoods you can look at, what sort of mortgage you will apply for, and what you will tell your real estate professional. So figuring out your price range is critical.

There are two questions to answer when determining your price range: How much of a down payment do you have, and how much can you borrow? Of course you probably already know how much money you have to put down. It may be $7,500 or it may be $75,000. What you don't know yet is whether that should equal 5 percent of the home, or 10 or 20 percent. A $7,500 down payment is 5 percent of a $150,000 home, which means that you would need to borrow $142,500. Can you afford a $142,500 mortgage? That's the question you need to answer.

The amount of home you can afford depends upon a variety of factors:

Your Income—The mortgage lender will need to know what you currently earn and what you will likely be earning over the life of the loan.

Down Payment—The more money you can put down on a home, the more expensive a home you can buy, or the lower your monthly payments will be. You also may be able to afford a home in a more desirable location.

Monthly Payments—How much can you afford to pay each month? The more you can come up with for your monthly mortgage payment, the more expensive a home you can afford. Traditionally, lenders have expected homebuyers to spend no more than 28 percent of their gross monthly income on mortgage payments, taxes, and insurance, although some lenders allow as much as 32 percent to go for these items.

Existing Debt—How much debt do you have already? The less, the better. When lenders decide how large a mortgage you qualify for, they use two ratios to determine your ongoing ability to make your mortgage payments. First, they look at how much of your income your home payments will require (your housing ratio). Second, they look at how much of your income will be used to pay off all debt, including the mortgage, credit cards, car loans, and so forth (your debt ratio). Lenders prefer that your total monthly debt payments account for no more than about 36 percent of your gross monthly income.

Interest Rate—The lower the prevailing interest rate, the more home you can afford. Interest rates can make a significant difference in your monthly payments. For instance, on a 30-year, $120,000 mortgage at 10 percent interest, you would pay about $1,050 per month, not including taxes and insurance. At 6 percent interest, you would pay only about $719 per month. Or, to put it an-

fast fact

smart step

When deciding on a mortgage, be sure to factor in your long-term financial goals, including saving for college and retirement.

other way, $1,050 a month would buy you a $175,000 home at 6 percent interest, but only a $120,000 home at 10 percent interest.

Length of the Loan—You can buy a more expensive home if you are willing to take on a longer mortgage. Most mortgages are for fifteen, twenty, or thirty years. A 15-year mortgage is paid off more quickly—and saves thousands of dollars in interest charges—but the monthly payments are higher. You may not be able to afford the home you want with a 15-year mortgage, but it might work out with a 20- or 30-year mortgage.

The Neighborhood—Home prices vary considerably from one neighborhood to another. You may not be able to afford a home in your favorite neighborhood initially, but home prices in more desirable neighborhoods generally increase faster than in less desirable neighborhoods. Once you've built up some equity in the first home you purchase, you may be able to sell it to generate a larger down payment for a home in a more desirable neighborhood.

We will walk you through the home-loan process in detail in the next chapter, but at this point you need a ballpark figure of how large a mortgage for which you may be able to qualify. One simple way to figure it out is to look at your housing and debt ratio.

For a conventional mortgage (such as a 30-year fixed loan), lenders typically want to see ratios of no more than 28/36; that is, they want your housing ratio, the percentage of your income that goes toward your home payments, to be 28 percent or less of your gross monthly income. They also want to see that your debt ratio, or the percentage of your income that goes toward your home payment plus your other debts, does not exceed 36 percent of your gross monthly income.

YOUR HOUSING RATIO

Your monthly home payments (Principal, Interest, Taxes, and Insurance, or PITI) divided by your gross monthly income equals your housing ratio.

PITI $_____ ÷ Monthly Income $_____ = _____ Your Housing Ratio

EXAMPLE:

Monthly payments (PITI):	$1,120
Monthly income:	$4,000
Your Housing Ratio:	.28

$1,120 ÷ $4,000 = .28 × 100 = 28.0%

YOUR DEBT RATIO

Monthly home payments (PITI) plus your monthly payments on other debt equals your total monthly debt payments. Your total monthly debt payments divided by your gross monthly income equals your debt ratio.

PITI $_____ + Other Monthly Debt Payments $_____ = $_____ Total Monthly Debt Payments

Total Monthly Debt Payments $_____ ÷ Monthly Income $_____ = _____ Your Debt Ratio

EXAMPLE:

Monthly payments (PITI):	$1,120
+	
Monthly payments on other debt:	$ 320
=	
Your total debt payments:	$1,440
÷	
Your monthly income:	$4,000
=	
Your Debt Ratio:	.36

$1,440 ÷ $4,000 = .36 × 100 = 36%

fast fact

Mortgage is a word that comes from 13th-century France. "Mort" means death, and "gage" means pledge. So a mortgage is, literally, a death pledge.

Here's another way to determine how large a mortgage payment you can afford based on your current financial situation.

1. **Determine your monthly gross income.**

2. **Multiply your monthly gross income by .28.** The result is the higher end of a mortgage payment you could qualify for using a conventional loan.

3. **Multiply your gross monthly income by .36.** The result is the higher end of an amount of total monthly debt payment you can have. From this number, subtract your normal monthly payments, including car loans or credit card payments. The result is the amount you can spend on a mortgage.

Let's take a look at an example.

HOW MUCH MORTGAGE CAN TOM AND KAYLA AFFORD?

Tom and Kayla earn $5,000 per month and have $800 in other monthly debt expense (automobile loan and credit card debt). How large of a mortgage payment can they afford?

Gross monthly income multiplied by .28 (housing ratio): $5,000 x .28 = $1,400.

The higher end of a mortgage payment they *could* qualify for is $1,400.

Gross monthly income multiplied by .36 (debt ratio): $5,000 x .36 = $1,800.

The higher end of their total debt, including mortgage payments, *could be* $1,800.

To determine how much mortgage they would actually qualify for, subtract their monthly debt payments from this amount:

$1,800 – $800 = $1,000

So $1,000 is the higher end of a monthly mortgage payment that Tom and Kayla could afford.

How does this translate into how much home you can afford? One rule of thumb is that you may be able to qualify for a home of up to 2.5 times your annual salary. This figure gives you an estimate of what you can afford, but there are a number of other factors to consider, such as how your other monthly debt may impact this number. For example, if you earn $60,000 annually, the rule of thumb would suggest that you could purchase a home with a value of about $150,000 ($60,000 x 2.5). However, this ignores other factors such as any other monthly debt obligations that you may have and does not take into account any funds you may be able to use for a down payment. Your best bet is to discuss your financial situation with your mortgage lender to better understand how much home you can qualify for and how much you actually want to spend.

Preapproval

Before you shop for a home, shop for a lender. This step can make it much easier to purchase the home you want. Once you find a lender that offers a good interest rate with acceptable terms, ask that lender to preapprove you for a mortgage.

Preapproval is the first step in the process to obtaining final approval. You fill out some forms detailing your income, assets, and debts. The lender looks over your forms, reviews your credit history, and determines how much they will approve for your loan based upon the information you provide.

A preapproval is not a commitment to lend, and the loan officer who preapproves you does not make the final approval. But once you are preapproved, you can shop with confidence for the homes in your price range without wasting your time on homes that don't fit into your financial picture.

fast fact

If more than 36 percent of your net pay is earmarked for debt, including your home mortgage, then you are probably spending above your means. Cut back on your expenses and reduce your debt.

It is sometimes possible to qualify for a loan amount that is more than you can afford. Be sure the amount of your mortgage actually makes sense for your personal financial situation.

You may be given a preapproval letter that you will be able to show when you submit a bid for a home. With it, the seller is more likely to accept your bid over one from a potential buyer who has not been preapproved.

Finding Money for the Down Payment

The hardest part of buying a home for most people is coming up with the down payment. A 20 percent down payment can be a considerable amount of money. On a $100,000 home, a 20 percent down payment is $20,000, and on a $250,000 home, a 20 percent down payment is $50,000. It's difficult to save that kind of money—particularly while you're paying rent, buying a car, and raising a family.

Here is how some new homeowners have covered their down payment:

Parents—It is not unusual for new homebuyers to get a portion of their down payment from parents or other relatives. If you are lucky enough to have your family help you out, good for you.

Inheritance—Have you inherited money from a parent or relative? Do you expect to inherit in the future? Put any inheritance away in an untouchable account, and use it to help with the down payment.

Federal Government—The federal government offers several programs designed to help new homebuyers. Both the Federal Housing Administration (FHA) and the Department of Veterans Affairs (VA) make available loan programs that require little or no money down for first-time homebuyers and veterans. Ask your lender if you qualify. Lenders administer the loans, so they will know if you are eligible and how to apply. Also, the Rural Housing Service (RHS) offers low-interest loans to people who live in rural areas or small towns.

State Governments—Some states offer help for first-timers. Again, lenders should be familiar with what is available for you.

Fannie Mae, Freddie Mac, and Ginnie Mae—Three corporations that were created by Congress can help you get a better mortgage. Fannie Mae (the Federal National Mortgage Association), Freddie Mac (the Federal Home Loan Mortgage Corporation), and Ginnie Mae (the Government National Mortgage Association) assist people with low or moderate incomes. Although these corporations are not consumer-direct lenders, qualified lenders can help you apply for loan products created by these organizations. If you qualify, it could mean not only a lower down payment but also a lower interest rate.

Investments—Some lenders allow you to use your stocks and bonds as collateral to qualify for a home loan with less money up front.

Retirement Savings—Your retirement savings generally should not be touched for any reason other than retirement. However, a home can be such a great investment that you might consider tapping into your retirement fund to make it possible to buy one. If you have an IRA, you can withdraw up to $10,000 penalty-free to buy a first home. The amount you include in your income depends on whether the IRA is a Roth IRA or traditional IRA and, if a traditional IRA, whether you have made nondeductible contributions. Be sure to consult your tax professional before making a withdrawal to determine what taxes and penalties may apply.

Your lender should be able to guide you through the various options to find a down payment solution that is right for you. Remember, if you can't afford a 20 percent down payment, you may be required to buy private mortgage insurance, which serves as a guarantee to the lender that if you don't pay, the insurance company will pay for any loss (up to a certain amount) experienced by the lender after foreclosure. Buying private mortgage insurance is expensive and

smart step

Start now!

Determine your monthly mortgage payment for any amount.

Log on to
hrblock.com/advisor

can add dramatically to the cost of paying for your home. But it does allow you
to buy a home with a down payment of as little as 3 to 5 percent.

Working with Real Estate Professionals

In Chapter 4 we will discuss the details of finding and working with real estate
professionals. It is important to know that finding a real estate professional
with whom you can work should happen early in the process and is an important part of putting together a good home buying plan.

Real estate professionals perform all sorts of tasks that can make your home
buying process easier and more pleasant. Aside from helping you locate the
right home, they can help you narrow down your choices to the right neighborhood, help make the right offer for the right price, and assist with the closing. So it makes sense to consider them an important part of your overall plan.

Location, Location, Location

The next step in your home buying plan should be coming up with an idea
of where you want to purchase a home, if you don't already know. Deciding where you want to live is not necessarily a simple matter. Many different and important considerations must be taken into account, such as:

The Community—The community that you will be working, living, and playing
in is almost as important as the actual home you are going to buy. Don't underestimate how different various communities are. People, homes, values, and
lifestyles are much different in, say, New York City than they are in Oklahoma
City. They can even vary from neighborhood to neighborhood within a city. So
you need to find a community in which you will be comfortable; you want your

desires to be in sync with this new area if it is to become your home. Some general factors you might want to consider are:

- **The quality of the school district** (if you have or will be having children; school quality also impacts resale value)
- **The socioeconomic aspects of various areas** (stability, growth)
- **Resale value of homes** (appreciation of value)
- **Services** (access to the things you need)
- **Commute times** (time required to get from place to place)

Specifically, you'll want to consider:

The Climate—Hot summers? Rainy springs? Snowy winters? You need to decide what is important to you and what you can live with. Find out what the averages are as well as the extremes.

The Financial Stability of the Area—Is the area dependent upon a major employer, and if so, is that employer likely to stay? What about the tax structure? Do residents support taxes and services or not? Is the economy strong? Learning about and understanding the local economy is vital; you certainly don't want to move across the country to an unfamiliar area only to learn that its economy was devastated when all the jobs in a specific industry that the economy depended on disappeared.

The Quality of Life—Does the area have a sense of community? Do people seem friendly? Can you walk around safely at night? Are there things to do on weekends? What sort of recreational options are available? Are there places of worship from which to choose? Having a great home in an area that doesn't fit your lifestyle makes no sense.

Other Intangibles of the Area—This may be the hardest thing to figure out from a distance. Different areas have different value systems. It is important to

smart step

You may be able to borrow money for your down payment from your retirement plan at work. Contact your plan administrator to find out if this option is available to you and, if so, whether you meet the requirements.

understand the values that are present in the area you are going to be living in and pick a place where values are similar to your own or where you can accept and live with the differences that do exist.

If you are looking to buy a home in an area you know, you have probably already considered these and other factors. If, on the other hand, you are moving to a new community, these are factors you need to look at. As mentioned, your real estate professional should prove to be a valuable resource. There are several other ways to learn about a community different from the one in which you are now living:

- **Read the local paper.** You can probably find it online. Local concerns, letters to the editor, and major news stories will tell you much about the values, attitudes, and issues in different areas.
- **Contact the chamber of commerce.** The local chamber will be happy to send you information about the community.
- **Talk to the locals.** What do they like and dislike about the area?

The Neighborhood

After you narrow your search to a particular area, you need to narrow it even further to a particular neighborhood. Finding the right one is important, but can be time-consuming. You need to drive around to see what each neighborhood has to offer. If you think it may be the right neighborhood, get out of the car and walk around, too. The only way to get a feel for a neighborhood is to spend time there, walk around, talk to the residents, and drive to the stores. Make sure this neighborhood feels right to you, will be convenient for you, and has the services you need.

There will likely be several neighborhoods that will be interesting to you. Look around some more. Is pride of ownership in the other homes evident? How

THE CHALLENGE

Sarah and David, both in their mid-thirties, have lived most of their lives in the Seattle area. Sarah's employer is consolidating its operations to a more centralized location in Kansas City. This seems like a good career move for Sarah, and both Sarah and David are open to living somewhere else. Their children are young enough to be moved easily, so Sarah and David begin to look at relocating to a new community.

Sarah and David read the local papers online and request information from the chamber of commerce. One of the first things they find is that there are two cities named Kansas City, one in the state of Missouri and the other in the state of Kansas, separated by the state line. It also seems there are many communities they need to consider in the suburbs surrounding the city. But the area is so big that they have no specific idea about where they want to live.

THE PLAN

Sarah and David hire a real estate professional who is recommended by Sarah's coworkers in the new office. The agent shows the couple different areas and neighborhoods, but none feel quite right. Some neighborhoods have good schools but are far away from downtown, while others seem nice but do not have many children. The couple worry that buying a home in an area they don't know well could be a recipe for disaster.

Finally, Sarah comes up with an answer. She decides that the family should move to an area that seems right and *rent* for a year. The family can take the time to learn if they really like the community enough to settle there, and if not, they will likely discover an area they do like. The couple follows Sarah's plan. Almost every weekend, they explore the metropolitan area, looking at different neighborhoods.

A year later, Sarah and David are happy with their decision. In that year, they found a neighborhood that they love. Renting for a year gave them the chance to find the right spot. They looked for homes in that area, found the right one, put in an offer, and moved in once their lease ended.

available is public transportation? What do the parks and schools look like? Is traffic an issue?

It is especially important to research home sales in the area. You want to find out:

- **The average selling price**
- **The amenities and size for homes that you can afford**
- **Whether there was a large disparity between the selling price and the asking price**

One source for this information is the Internet. By typing your requirements into your favorite search engine, you can find homes in the area that match your desires. You can find out what home sales look like, how strong the market is, and what you can expect to get for what you can afford.

The trick is to find a neighborhood you can afford, where home values are appreciating, with services that you find important, that is not too far from where you work or will work, and that has the look and feel you like.

Narrowing the Choices

D eciding upon the right community and even the right neighborhood is a fine start. Now you need to narrow your focus once again. What is it that you want and need in that perfect home that is out there somewhere waiting for you?

Buying a home is like buying a new television. It is unlikely that you would ever go shopping without having at least some idea of what it is you are looking for. Do you want a 65-inch high-definition projection television for the recreation room or a 13-inch VCR combination for the children's room?

The same holds true as you begin your home search. In Chapter 5, we discuss the many different kinds of dwellings available to you, including new and used homes, condos and town homes, and so forth. But before you get to that part of the decision-making process, you need to think now about what you want and need in your perfect home.

One of the very first things to do is to distinguish between your wants and needs. Hunting for a home takes a lot of time, and if you don't have a good idea about what is important and what is not, you may make the process even longer. So you need to determine what it is that you want and what you absolutely need. It is important to remember that although a home may not have everything you want, it may be possible to add those things later.

It is not uncommon for people to fall in love with a home or an area but to later realize that, like the child who puts too much food on his or her plate, their eyes are bigger than their stomachs. Few things are more disappointing than overestimating what you can do home-wise and then realizing that you may still be several years and a few moves away from owning your dream home. So begin by deciding what is essential and what is not.

fast fact

In 1884, the heiress of the Winchester Rifle fortune, Sarah L. Winchester, began construction on her dream home. It took 38 years to complete the 160-room mansion.

WANTS VERSUS NEEDS	
WHAT YOU MAY WANT	**YOU MAY ACTUALLY NEED**
Master bedroom suite	3 bedrooms
Whirlpool tub	2 bathrooms
Wooden deck or gazebo	Fenced-in backyard
A kitchen island	A dishwasher
A 3-car garage	Covered parking
A loft space	A basement
A short commute	A good school district

smart step

Consider the importance of the local economy in your choice of areas. Ask yourself if the community will still be desirable seven years from now.

In all likelihood, you will find several homes that combine your needs with some of your wants. Finding a home that meets all your requirements may or may not happen. So some of the things you need to consider as you prepare your wants/needs list are:

- **What does the present hold?** How big a home do you need? How many square feet and how many bedrooms? Do you need a home office? Do you need a room near the master bedroom for a nursery?
- **What does the future hold?** You need to think about not only what your needs are today, but what they are likely to be in a few years. Will you be having children? Is your job one that you will be staying with? If so, what kind of commute do you want?
- **How long do you plan on living in the home?** A home is usually a long-term investment, but not always. Most people stay in a home for an average of seven years. If you plan on living in this place for a shorter amount of time, you need to be concerned about resale value.

Beyond these broad considerations, you also want to consider some specific information about the home and community. The way a home will be used can be as unique as the individual homeowner.

Some Factors for You to Consider:

You may also have factors unique to your personal situation that are not listed. If a factor is important to you, make sure you consider it *before* buying your home.

- **Type of home:** single family, multifamily, town home, condominium, co-op, mobile home, etc.
- **Style of home:** one story, multistory, colonial, traditional, etc.
- **Age of home:** new construction, previously owned (newer, or older)
- **Size of home:** square footage

- **Floor plan of home:** location of rooms (does it fit your lifestyle and needs), number of bedrooms and bathrooms, other rooms (den, family room, etc.), stairs, etc.
- **Amenities of home:** garage (for how many vehicles), basement, appliances, central air-conditioning, fireplace, built-in features (such as bookcases), flooring (carpet, hardwood floors, tile, etc.), energy-efficient features (windows, doors, etc.), security features, etc.
- **Outdoor features of home**: yard (size), landscaping, pool or spa, fencing, views surrounding the home, exterior lighting, etc.
- **Special features of the home:** handicap accessible, other physical needs, etc.
- **Community features of the home:** schools, homeowners' association, restrictive covenants, clubhouse, community pool, golf course, access to transportation, etc.

Patience Is a Virtue

Finding the right home can be a long, time-consuming, tiring process, even when you know exactly what you want. Why? Because once you know what it is you are looking for, it is difficult to settle for less. Some people drive by hundreds of homes and look inside scores of them before finding the right one.

The process of finding a home can also be very stressful. What if someone finds that home before you do? What if a home goes on the market and you don't see it? There are many things you could worry about, but why do so? All your worry won't make any difference in the end. We are sure you will find a home you love. So enjoy the process, because it can, and hopefully will, result in you getting the home of your dreams.

Before you apply for a loan, before you hire a real estate professional, before you even start to drive around, you'll want to have a fairly good idea about

fast fact

Home sales are an important indicator of how the economy is doing. So-called new home starts measure the number of new home construction start-ups in any given annual quarter.

smart step

Don't under-estimate the importance of your home's floor plan. It determines where you will be eating, sleeping, and relaxing. A bad floor plan can definitely interfere with your lifestyle.

what kind of home you want, at what price, and in what neighborhood. By creating a home buying plan you will know what you can afford, what you need in a home and in a real estate professional, and how much of a loan you must get.

the ESSENTIALS

1 A home buying plan is your first step in the process of purchasing a home. It is your map for where you want to go and how you are going to get there.

2 Figuring out how much you can afford to spend on a home is based on factors such as the amount of your down payment, the interest rate, the length of the mortgage loan, how much money you make, and your current debt load.

3 Choosing the right community takes a lot of homework. You want to be sure that the area will fit the lifestyle you desire.

4 Narrowing your choice to the right neighborhood can take hours of research and looking around to find just the right one for you.

5 Knowing what it is you are looking for in a home will make the process of finding one that much easier. Understand the difference between your wants and needs.

3

FINDING THE MONEY:
Exploring Your Mortgage Options

"Money often costs too much."

—Ralph Waldo Emerson

William Randolph Hearst began building his home, Hearst Castle, in 1919. Among other attributes, it was once home to the world's largest private zoo, with zebras, camels, giraffes, and kangaroos.

One of the great things about buying a home is that you only need to come up with a small part of the money necessary to make the purchase. If you can save 5 or 10 percent, you should be able to get a mortgage lender or other financial institution to lend you the rest. Finding a lender takes work and you may be taking on significant debt, but the good news is that your mortgage can help you make one of your dreams a reality.

Good Debt and Bad Debt

If going into debt to buy a home makes you nervous, a bit of a pep talk might be in order. The first thing to understand is that not all debt is bad debt. Debt allows you to do things you otherwise could not do, such as start a business, go to college, or pay for a home. Debt constructs buildings and funds investments. Entire corporations and even the government are funded by debt. The important thing is to take on good debt and avoid bad debt.

What's the difference between good debt and bad debt? Debt that helps you, that enriches your life, that is manageable, and that is not a burden is good debt. For example, student loans are good debt if they enabled you to get through school and further your life goals. They are bad debt if you dropped out of medical school after one year to become a writer. A good debt helps; a bad debt hinders.

To Borrow or Not to Borrow

Put simply, whenever you use credit, you're borrowing money that has to be paid back. It's important for you to know when it is wise to borrow and when it isn't. Sometimes you can save money instead of borrowing.

It's a good idea to borrow for the following (if you need to):

- **A home that might increase in value**
- **Home improvements that will increase your home's value**

- **A college education**
- **A reliable car**

You may need to borrow for these items, but pay the debt back as soon as possible:
- **Uninsured medical bills**
- **Family emergencies** (for example, to attend a relative's funeral)
- **Household emergencies** (for example, the furnace breaks down in winter)

Do not borrow for the following (wait until you can pay cash):
- **Vacations**
- **New furniture**
- **Electronic equipment**
- **Boats and motorcycles**
- **Entertainment equipment**

Gifts from relatives may sometimes be included in your down payment, but if so, they must be disclosed to the lender.

Bad debts cause stress. You sleep poorly because of them. They can cause fights and foster guilt. Supreme Court Justice Lewis Powell was once asked to define *obscenity*. Hard-pressed to come up with a definition, Powell uttered the famous line, "I know it when I see it." The same could be said for bad debt: You know it when you see it, and it can certainly be obscene in how it impacts your personal financial situation.

A mortgage should not just be considered a good debt; it can usually be considered a great debt. Not only will it permit you to own your own home, but it also allows you to build equity and receive significant tax breaks. It is almost always a smart financial choice and a wise debt to take on.

Understanding Mortgages

Before you learn about the different types of mortgage loans available, it is wise to first understand what your mortgage payment will consist of so you know what it is you will be shopping for. There are four parts to a mortgage payment. Combined, they are called PITI: Principal, Interest, Taxes, and Insurance.

1. **Principal**—This is the actual amount you borrow. If your dream home costs $150,000 and you want to borrow $142,500 and pay $7,500 out of pocket, the $142,500 is the principal amount of your loan.

2. **Interest**—This is what it will cost you to borrow the principal. It is expressed as a percentage—the interest rate—and is paid as part of your monthly payment. If you borrow $142,500 at 7 percent for thirty years, you will pay $198,800 of interest over the lifetime of the mortgage.

3. **Taxes**—Each year, your county and/or city assesses your property and you must pay a tax on the **assessed** value. This may be included in your mortgage payment or you may be able to pay your local government directly.

4. **Insurance**—Your lender will require that the property be properly insured. Insurance will be discussed in detail in Chapter 11, but it is important at this point to understand that the term insurance may be describing two different types of insurance. Homeowner's insurance provides coverage for the property in case it is damaged or destroyed, and it protects you and the lender. Private mortgage insurance (PMI) protects the lender (if you are required to pay it) should you default on the mortgage.

Aside from these four things, there are two other aspects of getting a home loan that you need to understand.

1. **Down payment**—As discussed previously, depending upon the loan you apply for, your down payment will be anywhere from 0 percent (with a Veteran's Administration loan) on up. Most homebuyers put down between 5 and 15 percent.

    If you can afford a significant down payment, it usually is a good idea to make one. The benefits of making a large down payment are twofold. First, it reduces the principal amount borrowed and consequently your monthly mortgage payment. Second, when you pay 20 percent or more, you are not required to pay private mortgage insurance, further reducing your monthly payment.

plain talk

The value of your property assigned by your local taxing authority is its assessed value. This value is not necessarily its market value (the amount you could receive if you sold it).

2. **Closing costs**—You must also figure closing costs into your financing equation. Closing costs are expenses over and above your down payment. They include costs associated with obtaining a loan (such as points, credit reports, title insurance, and so forth), costs associated with establishing and transferring ownership of the property (such as recording fees and transfer taxes), and costs of items that need to be paid to state and local governments. They normally amount to between 2 and 5 percent of the loan amount and are paid at the time of closing. For example, if you take out a $150,000 loan, you could expect your closing costs to add up to between $3,000 and $7,500. We'll discuss the details of closing more in Chapter 10.

Common Mortgage Types

Buying a home involves making one decision after another: How much home can you afford? What neighborhood do you like? What kind of house do you want? Equally important are the money decisions. What sort of loan is best for you? Which lender? There are numerous mortgage possibilities. Let's begin to narrow the field.

Fixed-Rate Mortgages (FRM)—Fixed-rate mortgages are generally offered as a 15-, 20-, or 30-year loan. As the name implies, the interest rate for this loan is fixed, so you have the comfort of knowing exactly what your monthly mortgage payment will be, no matter how interest rates change in the future. If rates are good and you plan on being in the home for several years, fixed-rate loans can make a lot of sense.

Adjustable-Rate Mortgages (ARM)—Adjustable-rate mortgages usually carry an interest rate that is somewhat lower than fixed-rate mortgages. A lower rate can help lower your monthly payments. The adjustable rate may be "fixed" for a few years, so you can be assured of having low mortgage payments for the

fast fact

When lenders require less money for a down payment, borrowers have less equity in the home and the likelihood of default increases. PMI provides protection for the lender in case of default.

smart step

Start Now!

Determine whether a fixed-rate or adjustable-rate mortgage is better for you.

Log on to
hrblock.com/advisor

FIXED-RATE MORTGAGE (FRM)	
ADVANTAGES	**DISADVANTAGES**
■ Interest rates and payments stay the same (even if interest rates increase). You can manage your money easily because you know in advance what your mortgage payment will be. Your monthly mortgage payment may change a little from year to year, due to changes in property taxes and insurance costs on your home, but the total cost of interest and principal will stay exactly the same each month for the entire 15-, 20-, or 30-year life of the loan. ■ It is easy to understand.	■ You can't take advantage of falling interest rates unless you refinance, which involves time and money (in the form of closing costs related to the refinanced loan). ■ It can be expensive if you're borrowing during a time of high interest rates. ■ The mortgage can't be customized for you except in terms of length (15-, 20-, or 30-year). Fixed-rate mortgages are generally the same from lender to lender. ■ It is harder to qualify for a fixed-rate loan. The initial payment might be lower on an adjustable-rate mortgage due to a lower interest rate.

fixed term of the loan. After the fixed term, the lender is permitted to adjust the interest rate periodically as outlined in the terms of the loan, meaning your payments can change as interest rates change. A cap limits how much the interest rate or monthly payment can change based on the terms of the loan.

The Length of the Loan

The second part of the mortgage equation has to do with the length (or term) of the loan. The typical loan length is fifteen, twenty, or thirty years. A 30-year loan is good because it lowers your monthly payment, but the overall cost of borrowing the money is higher because you pay more in total interest charges to borrow for a longer period of time. The payment for a 15-year loan is more every month, but you pay dramatically less interest over

ADJUSTABLE-RATE MORTGAGE (ARM)

- Early in the loan, you'll have lower rates and payments than with a fixed-rate mortgage.

- If interest rates go down, your mortgage payment will go down.

- Adjustable-rate mortgages are easier to qualify for because interest rates and payment amounts are lower than with fixed mortgages.

- You may be able to purchase a larger home than you might with a fixed-rate mortgage.

- Lenders can be flexible in determining the features of the loan, such as the caps and the adjustment index.

- If you are not planning to live in the home very long, an adjustable-rate mortgage may offer a more economical way to buy a home.

- If your payment is lower than it would be with a fixed-rate mortgage, you can save the extra money for another financial goal.

- The interest rate and associated payments can increase over the life of the loan. There are caps to the increases, but your payment may increase significantly if interest rates rise significantly. The **annual percentage rate** (APR) for an ARM is a moving target because neither you nor the lender can predict what the interest rate will be in the future.

- An adjustable-rate mortgage can be harder to understand than a fixed-rate mortgage.

- If your payment on the loan is set too low or if there is a payment cap, you can end up owing more money than you did when you closed on the loan (this is called negative amortization). That happens because your monthly payment doesn't cover all of the interest due, and the unpaid interest is added to your principal.

- Your interest rate will be adjusted annually or more often. The rate on an adjustable-rate mortgage may soon be higher than the rate on a fixed-rate mortgage.

- You can refinance to get into a fixed-rate mortgage, but it may be at a higher rate and you'll incur refinancing costs.

- If you qualified for a house based on a low interest payment and rates go up, the house may no longer be so affordable.

plain talk

The annual percentage rate (APR) includes not only the interest rate you are being charged, but also any fees and other charges incurred in obtaining the loan.

If you don't qualify for a 15-year mortgage (and if your loan carries no pre-payment penalties), you can still knock about six years off of your 30-year mortgage by paying just one extra mortgage payment every year.

the course of the loan. A 20-year loan will be somewhere in between a 15- and 30-year loan, with lower payments than on a 15-year loan and less interest paid than on a 30-year loan. Loans of shorter length have a higher payment every month, so they are harder to qualify for. But consider their value:

TOTAL INTEREST COSTS			
Term of loan	30 years	20 years	15 years
Amount borrowed	$150,000	$150,000	$150,000
Interest rate*	7%	7%	7%
Total interest paid	$209,263	$129,107	$92,683

*Interest rates generally vary with the term of loan. Example illustrates the effect of different lengths of loans.

Balloon Mortgage—If you can't afford a big down payment, you might be able to get a balloon mortgage. With a balloon mortgage, you pay a little up front, followed by several years of monthly payments, followed by a "balloon" payment that pays the entire remaining loan balance. A balloon mortgage might work if you expect to move, refinance, or receive a big chunk of money from work or family that would cover the balloon payment. Generally, a homeowner refinances just before the balloon payment is due. By taking out a traditional mortgage when the balloon payment is due, the homeowner is able to avoid the balloon payment.

Common Mortgage Programs

Now you know the difference between a fixed-rate mortgage and an adjustable-rate mortgage and the details of 15-, 20-, and 30-year mortgages. Next up: Understanding common loan types. With each of the loans discussed next you can opt for an FRM (15, 20, or 30 years) or an ARM.

Conventional—This is the traditional loan. It is not insured or guaranteed by U.S. government agencies such as Housing and Urban Development (HUD), the Federal Housing Administration (FHA), or the Department of Veterans Affairs (VA).

FHA Loans—The FHA is a division of HUD. The federal government knows how important home ownership is to the American economy and for social stability, so it has the FHA guarantee certain loans to make home ownership more attainable.

Generally, FHA loans are for low- and middle-income borrowers, as well as first-time buyers. FHA loan amounts vary by county and are usually easier to qualify for than conventional mortgage loans because the federal government guarantees them. Other advantages may include a smaller down payment being required and the opportunity to have the mortgage include closing costs and fees.

VA Loans—VA loans are just about the best home mortgage deals available, so if you can qualify for one, do so. VA loans are made by private mortgage lenders, and are guaranteed by the Veteran's Administration. You must intend to occupy the home that the loan is used to purchase. If you are eligible and meet other requirements, the terms are quite reasonable, with limited closing costs. It is even possible to get a loan with no down payment. The loan can also be for up to 100 percent of the reasonable value (established by the VA) of the home, although VA lenders generally limit VA loans to $240,000. Because the federal government guarantees VA loans, banks are more willing to loan money to people with previous credit problems.

VA loans are available to veterans of World War II, Korea, Vietnam, the Gulf War, and selected reserves, as well as members of the National Guard, peace-time veterans, and members of certain other organizations. If you are not sure if you qualify, you can apply for a Certificate of Eligibility by using VA Form 26-1880, Request for a Certificate of Eligibility for Home Loan Benefits, and submitting it to one of the VA Eligibility Centers.

smart step

Start Now!

Determine your monthly mort-gage payment and the amount of interest you'll pay over the lifetime of the loan.

Log on to
hrblock.com/advisor

Rural Housing Service—The Rural Housing Service (RHS) is an agency of the U.S. Department of Agriculture (USDA) and facilitates home ownership among low- and moderate-income rural Americans. Some options include low-cost loans direct from RHS or loan guarantees to private lenders for up to 100 percent of the appraised value, eliminating the need for a down payment. To find out if you are eligible, contact your Rural Development State Office.

Fannie Mae, Freddie Mac, and Ginnie Mae—If money is tight, three corporations that were created by Congress can help you get a better mortgage. Fannie Mae (the Federal National Mortgage Association), Freddie Mac (the Federal Home Loan Mortgage Corporation), and Ginnie Mae (the Government National Mortgage Association) assist people with low or moderate incomes. Although these are not consumer-direct lenders, qualified lenders can help you apply for loans from these organizations. If you qualify, it could mean not only a lower down payment but also a lower interest rate.

No-Document Loans (Also Known as "Stated Income")—No document or stated income loans are loans that require little documentation to back up the information contained in your loan application. As such, they are generally used by the self-employed who may make a lot of money, but who also have many deductions on their tax returns, or whose income may fluctuate from year to year. Loans of this type rely on credit history and generally carry higher interest rates.

Selecting the Right Lender

Now comes decision time. From whom will you get the loan and what type of loan will it be? Remember that when shopping for a home loan, banks are not your only option. There are many different financial institutions that offer mortgages today, including:

- **Mortgage companies**
- **Banks**
- **Credit unions**
- **Trust companies**
- **Insurance companies**
- **Private lenders**
- **Other financial Institutions**

Keep in mind that you will want a lending institution that is large enough to get you the best deal but personal enough to appreciate your concerns. Find one that is experienced, trustworthy, and staffed with people with whom you can develop a good relationship. You'll want to find a lender that can fully evaluate your personal financial situation and offer you a loan product that is right for you. Remember, some lenders may not be able to offer all the loan products available and if you do business with that lender, you may have to settle for a loan that is good but not the best. What you are looking for is a lender that can offer you a wide array of choices and help you evaluate which is right for you.

Truth in Lending

The Truth in Lending Act (TILA) is a federal law that allows consumers to be more informed about the cost of credit. It requires that lenders fully disclose in writing the terms and conditions of a mortgage, including items such as the annual percentage rate (APR) and other charges, to help assure that consumers fully understand the difference in the cost of a credit versus a cash deal. The TILA also helps consumers to compare the cost of credit associated with different lenders. The lender must provide initial information within three business days of receipt of a written loan application and final information at or prior to closing the loan. The final version may be different because the APR and/or closing costs may change from what was calculated on the initial truth in lending (TIL) statement you received.

fast fact

A good loan officer is almost as important as a good lender. The loan officer should work to get you the best loan for your personal situation, and be your advocate within the lending institution.

If you are en-
rolled in one of
the U.S. military
academies or
you are a mem-
ber of certain
other organiza-
tions, such as
the Public
Health Service,
you may qualify
for a VA loan.

A TIL statement includes

- Contract reference
- Name and address of creditor
- Name and address of borrower
- Annual percentage rate (APR)
- Finance charge
- Amount financed
- Total of payments
- Total sale price
- Itemization of amount financed
- Payment term
- Demand feature
- Variable rate information (if applicable)
- Insurance requirements
- Security interest
- Security interest charges
- Filing fees
- Late charges
- Prepayment fee (if applicable)
- Assumption policy
- Required deposit information

If you selected an ARM, your lender should also provide you with a written sum-
mary of the terms and costs associated with the loan, information on the past
history of the index to which the rate will be tied, and a copy of the booklet
Consumer Handbook on Adjustable-Rate Mortgages. When you apply for a loan
to purchase your home, your lender should also provide you with a copy of
Settlement Costs: A HUD Guide, which describes the settlement process. The
TILA was intended to help you understand a mortgage and your rights along
the way.

The Application

Once you have selected a lender, you will need to provide a lot of information for your loan application, including:

- **Personal information.** Your lender will need to know your name, age, social security number, marital status, number of dependents, etc.
- **Your employer and your salary and bonuses.** Bring tax returns, pay stubs, and W-2 forms.
- **Other sources of income.** Including alimony, child support, investments, partnerships, lawsuits, and interest income.
- **Financial information.** Checking and savings accounts, stocks, bonds, mutual funds, other real estate, etc.
- **Your debts.** Monthly statements for credit cards, car loans, etc.
- **The property listing.** The lender will need to verify that the value of the property is appropriate for the loan you are requesting. The lender will require an independent appraisal of the home, which is discussed more in Chapter 9.

Freddie Mac, Fannie Mae, and Ginnie Mae are nicknames that are derived from the corporations' names and abbreviations (FHLMC, FNMA, GNMA).

What Lenders Want

Credit issuers—mortgage lenders, banks, credit-card companies, and other financial institutions—usually get a credit score from a credit source to help them determine your creditworthiness. Generally, there are certain key factors they examine:

- **Credit history**—Are you a recent convert to good credit, or have you always paid your bills on time? The longer your history of fiscal responsibility, the better your chances of being approved for additional debt.
- **Debt types**—Is your existing debt mostly consumer debt (charge cards and credit cards) or a home mortgage? The shorter your credit history, the more closely lenders look at your existing debt to make sure you are not overextended and your bills are being paid on time.

- **Existing debts**—The ratio of all your existing debt to your income is a key factor in determining the amount of additional credit you could receive.
- **Timely payments**—This factor is very important in a lender's eyes. If you pay your bills on time, you'll have a good chance of sailing smoothly through the loan application process. Unfortunately, this applies primarily to documented debt, such as credit cards, car payments, and mortgages. If you pay your rent and your utility bills on time, those payments are not likely to show up on your credit report. On the other hand, if you don't pay those bills on time, your tardiness could end up on your credit report.
- **Other credit applications**—If you've applied for credit frequently—especially recently—lenders get anxious. Even if you haven't run up large debts, lenders are always aware of the possibility that you could run up enough *other* debt to affect your ability to pay off *all* your debts.

Your ratings on these factors are run through computer models to calculate your **credit score**. In addition to your credit score, individual lenders take a close look at a few critical issues. For instance, it is a plus if you already own your home. If you have a good job, that's another plus. If you've been on that job and in that home for a few years, that's a huge plus. These facts show stability, dependability, equity, and, best of all, a steady income—all the attributes lenders look for in a loan applicant. On the other hand, if you're out of work, out of money, and behind on the rent, your chances of securing a loan are not promising.

If you have had credit problems in the past, don't hide from them. Be honest with the lender. Lenders have seen just about any problem a borrower can imagine, and many times over. There are so many loans available these days that it is likely your lender will be able to find one that works for you and your unique situation.

As you compare your options, it is easy to assume that the cheapest loan is probably the best loan. Sometimes that's true, and sometimes it's not. So as you shop for your mortgage, be sure to compare all the terms and conditions of the loans you are considering to ensure that you are making a fair and accurate comparison.

To Pay Points or Not to Pay Points, That Is the Question

As we discussed before, one point equals 1 percent of your loan amount and is paid to the lender at the closing. So paying no points certainly seems to be an attractive option, and we have all seen offers for loans with zero points. But is that really such a good idea?

Lenders offer zero-point loans because it is another way to get people into the home of their choice with a loan they can afford. On a $150,000 loan, one point equals $1,500. That can be a lot of money to come up with on top of your down payment. That is why zero-point loans are attractive; they allow buyers to get into homes without having to come up with any more cash. In exchange, you may have to pay a slightly higher interest rate, but if you get the home of your dreams, it can be worth it.

Of course you can't expect to get something for nothing, so if the lender isn't charging fees up front when it makes the loan, then it must make money somewhere else. Where is that? In your interest rate. The tradeoff for not paying points is that you will probably pay more over the term of the loan in interest charges.

A rule of thumb is to equate each point with ¼ (.25) percent interest rate. If you pay an extra point on a 7 percent mortgage, your rate will be lowered to about 6.75 percent. Is it worth it? That depends on how long you expect to stay in the home. If you plan to stay for many years, paying extra points up front might save you money in the long run. If, on the other hand, you expect to move to

**smart
step**

Look for a
lender who
provides great
customer service.
It will make the
loan process
go much more
smoothly.

another home in just a few years, you generally shouldn't pay the extra points. Your lender can help you determine whether paying extra points up front would be worthwhile for you.

Funding the Loan

The lender will review everything, including your loan application and supporting documentation. The loan underwriter may also check a few details—your employment, for example. The underwriter will then analyze the entire loan package and either approve it, deny it, or ask for more information.

A Word About Credit Reports

Lenders also look at the credit reports on which your score is based. Your credit report is your shadow personality. From the lender's perspective, the credit profile represents who you are and how you will probably behave with respect to the debt, if they lend you money. Your credit report contains basic information about you and also includes information about how you have handled past credit and debt, information on any liens, judgments, or bankruptcies, information about your current and past employers, and information about who else has been inquiring about your credit. If you are planning to apply for a mortgage, you will want to review your credit report and try to correct in advance anything that might be a problem or an error. You can order a copy of your credit report and credit score from any of the three major credit-reporting bureaus:

- **Equifax** (800–685–1111 or www.equifax.com)
- **Experian** (888–397–3742 or www.experian.com)
- **TransUnion** (800–888–4213 or www.transunion.com)

An explanation of how to read the report is included. You can also order a 3-in-1 report that merges reports from the three bureaus.

THE CHALLENGE

Brendan and Leslie are a young couple in their early thirties and have two small children. They are ready to buy their first home. They have $10,000 saved but are not sure how much they can afford to pay for a home. Before meeting with a real estate professional or looking at any houses, they first want to figure out what they can afford. The couple use the Internet to analyze their various mortgage options. They are surprised there are so many lenders and so many loan programs available. Confused by their many options, Brendan and Leslie have a hard time deciding what makes the most financial sense for them: points or no points, fifteen, twenty, or thirty years, conventional or stated income, and so forth. To make matters worse, everyone they talk to and everything they read seems to come to a different conclusion. "We don't know what to do," Brendan exclaims.

THE PLAN

Brendan and Leslie decide they need the help of an expert because they are not confident that they have the facts straight. After speaking with several mortgage lenders and asking around, they meet Ken, a loan officer who was highly recommended by some friends. Ken sits with the couple and listens to their needs and concerns. He takes the time to explain mortgage terms and options the couple didn't understand. Then, he draws up a profile of the couple's financial situation to develop a solution that is right for them.

Understanding that the couple has limited funds available for a down payment, Ken suggests they confine their home search to houses that meet local FHA guidelines. Because FHA loans can be had for as little as 3 percent down, this will preserve the couple's savings for closing costs, points, and maybe even some redecorating. Ken suggests that the couple take out a 30-year FRM (instead of a 15-year FRM) to reduce their monthly payment. He also suggests they consider paying points to reduce the interest rate and monthly payment.

This all makes sense to Brendan and Leslie. Initially, they were worried they might end up with a payment that would be a bit of a stretch every month, and they didn't like the uncertainty of knowing that their interest rate might increase if they chose an ARM. Ken's solution made the payments fit the couple's budget, and the FRM relieved their anxiety over changing interest rates. They were quite happy with Ken, because he took the time to find a solution that was right for them. The couple was even happier when their loan closed. "We got a great house at an affordable monthly payment and are looking forward to making this our home for a long time," Leslie remarked.

It is likely that your loan will come back with a conditional approval. Conditions range from providing extra documentation to verifying investments. It all depends on your loan program and your financial situation. Once all conditions have been met, final loan approval should come quickly, and all documents necessary to close the loan and the deal will be ordered. This entire process may happen in a few short days, or it may take many weeks or more.

After finding the right lender, the right loan, completing the paperwork, supplying all documentation, satisfying all conditions, and waiting, the end of the loan process is called settling up. The loan funds are not given to you directly but instead are wired to a neutral third party for safekeeping. Depending upon where you live, this could be a title company, an attorney, or an **escrow officer**. You then add in your share of the closing costs and the down payment, and all funds necessary to purchase the home should be on hand. The escrow officer wires the money to the seller's lender to pay off the seller's loan, all fees are paid, the seller gets whatever is left, you sign many papers (after reviewing them of course), and the deed to the house is recorded in your name.

As you can see, there are many options to consider and choices to be made when you are deciding how to finance the home of your dreams. Like many other decisions you'll have to make, you'll want to take the time to find the right lender, the right mortgage product, and the right terms to fit your personal financial situation.

plain talk

An escrow officer is a neutral third party (someone not directly involved in the transaction) who helps facilitate the transfer of money and property.

the ESSENTIALS

1 Not all debt is bad debt. If you manage debt effectively, it can help you acquire things, such as a home, over time.

2 Your mortgage payment generally consists of <u>P</u>rincipal, <u>I</u>nterest, <u>T</u>axes, and <u>I</u>nsurance (PITI).

3 Fixed- and adjustable-rate mortgages both have advantages and disadvantages. Determine which type of mortgage is better for your specific situation.

4 There are a variety of lenders and mortgages available today. Look for a lender that can help you fully evaluate all the available options and will work with you to get a mortgage that is right for you.

5 Paying points for a loan may or may not be right for you. Your mortgage lender can help you to determine which is the better option for your personal situation.

fast fact

Federal law prohibits lenders from giving different treatment or imposing different terms to applicants based on race, color, national origin, religion, sex, family status, or disability.

4 [SOME ASSISTANCE PLEASE: Working With Real Estate Professionals]

"Professionalism is knowing how to do it, when to do it, and doing it."

—Frank Tyger

Realtors® are agents or brokers who belong to the National Association of Realtors® and subscribe to the association's code of ethics.

Buying a home can be a complicated process. You need to find the right area with the right neighborhood that, of course, needs to have just the right home. Then there is the financing and inspections, not to mention the actual process of transferring ownership of the home to you. It's not easy, and the process can be painstaking and the legalities can be lengthy. With those thoughts in mind, you may find it helpful to enlist the services of an expert—a real estate professional.

Abraham Lincoln once remarked, "A man who represents himself has a fool for a client." We are not saying that you can't find and purchase a home on your own, but we are saying that you should consider the value that a real estate professional can add to the home-buying process. In this chapter, we will shed some light on the many roles of the real estate professional in the home-buying process. You may find that hiring a real estate professional makes sense for your personal situation.

Brokers, Agents, and Realtors®

Brokers, agents, and Realtors® have different roles. A broker is licensed by a state to own and run a real estate office. Brokers hire agents and get a percentage of the commission from every deal the agent closes. An agent *must* work for a broker in the real estate business. Brokers can (and do) act as agents—creating and closing deals—but it is important to understand that in any office, there is only one boss, and that is the broker.

A **Realtor**® (notice the capital R in this registered name) is an agent or broker who belongs to the National Association of Realtors®. Members must subscribe to the association's code of ethics, and in return they receive professional development, assistance with research, and an exchange of information among members.

Agents work for brokers and do most of the work in real estate sales. Your interactions will most likely be with the agent. Note, however, that there is more

ROLES OF AGENTS			
	BUYER'S AGENT	**SELLER'S AGENT**	**DUAL AGENT**
Represents	Buyer	Seller	Both parties, but tie goes to the seller
Wants buyers to pay	As little as possible	As much as possible	As much as possible
Paid by the	Seller	Seller	Seller
Conflict of interest?	No	No	Possible

smart step

Avoid agents who want to represent both sides of the transaction because you may end up paying more than necessary for the property.

than one kind of agent. Sellers of homes hire agents to list the property. Such agents are called *seller's* or *listing* agents. They can help you find a home that meets your needs, but they represent the seller's interests first, by getting the highest possible sales price, for example. Buyers of homes may want to consider hiring a *buyer's* agent, who represents the buyer's interests by finding the right home and negotiating the lowest price, for example.

Most agents will work on one side or the other of a sale. However, the seller's agent can also represent the buyer, acting as a so-called dual agent. The problem with dual agency is that the agent is contractually bound to get the highest price possible for the seller, so although he or she may be representing the buyer, too, the agent's true loyalties are with the seller.

It is possible to have one agent represent both sides, but it is not advisable. Buying a home is a negotiation. You want to buy the home for the lowest price possible, and the seller wants to sell it for the highest possible price. An agent representing both sides would have a conflict of interest. That may work against the buyer's interests because the agent normally gets a percentage of the sales price as a commission, so he or she has a vested interest in having the home sell for as much as possible. The smarter choice is to find an agent who will represent your interests alone. Sellers and buyers should have their own agents because a real estate transaction is like a two-way street.

A recent phenomenon is the discount broker who provides fewer services, but charges a smaller fee. The discount broker's primary role is to show you listings. When a home is listed for sale, it is posted for all agents and brokers to see on the **Multiple Listing Service** (MLS). Only real estate professionals have access to the MLS. A discount broker will get you onto the MLS so you can see what homes are available in your area for the price you want to pay. You then go it alone: you view the homes without the broker, you draft your own contracts, and so forth. In turn, the discount broker takes a much smaller fee, say 1 percent. By not using a full-service agent, you can generally knock off about 2 percent from your offer (see below). On a home of $150,000, that's $3,000.

Who Charges What?

Buyer's agents usually get a percentage of the sales price. Typically, 6 percent of the sale price is split evenly between the seller's agent and the buyer's agent. If you pay $150,000 for a home, then $9,000 of the seller's proceeds will go to the two agents, or $4,500 to each agent. As such, it is the

plain talk

The Multiple Listing Service (MLS) is an online database that lists all homes on the market, along with relevant information about each property.

TYPES OF REAL ESTATE PROFESSIONALS				
	BROKERS	AGENTS	REALTORS®	DISCOUNT BROKERS
Charge a commission	Yes	Yes	Yes	Yes, but generally less
Is a member of National Association of Realtors®	Maybe	Maybe	Yes	Maybe
Can hire other agents	Yes	No	Yes, if they are also a broker	Yes

seller who is really paying for both agents out of the proceeds from the sale of the home. In some areas, agents may require a **retainer**, but most do not.

Why You May Need an Agent

I t is understandable that you might not want an agent. You can, after all, offer less for a home if you don't have an agent. If the seller is paying only 3 percent for his agent and not the full 6 percent generally required when there are two agents, both the buyer and seller can save money.

But not using an agent may be shortsighted. Agents help people buy and sell property every day. Most people enter into only a few real estate transactions in their entire lives. An agent, on the other hand, should be familiar with all the details of the real estate transaction, which should be an asset to any buyer. Buying a home may be the largest financial investment you make during your lifetime. Hiring a professional so you are sure you are making intelligent decisions throughout the process only makes sense.

In addition, a buyer's agent can help you:

Find the Right Home—The agent will have access to the MLS, which alone is a valuable tool for buyers. The MLS can be sorted by price, number of bedrooms, areas, and so forth, so your agent will be able to pinpoint which homes are available in your price range in your desired area.

Once you have located a few homes you would like to see, your agent will call the listing agent, set up times to show you the homes, and then drive you around to the other homes on your list. When you get to each home, the agent will point out things about the home that you may not know about, for example, whether the decking may need to be redone, or the quality of schools in

plain talk

A retainer is a sum of money paid before services are performed for a client.

A contingency is a future event or condition upon which a valid contract is dependent. In other words, it's a hoop one side or the other *must* jump through to complete the deal.

the area. Your agent should tell you if the asking price for the home being offered is fair or not, and what a reasonable offer might be.

Understand the Finances—The finances of a home purchase and home ownership are not simple. A knowledgeable agent will understand the financial ins and outs of the transaction. For instance, he or she can narrow your search to appropriate homes based on your financial situation. Similarly, an agent can explain how much it costs to own a home, taking into account home maintenance, property taxes, insurance, and so on.

Negotiate a Great Deal—People who don't negotiate often are at a disadvantage when confronted with those who do. If you attempt to buy a home without using your own agent, you may end up paying too much, or you may not get the home at all. Real estate agents negotiate for a living. They know what homes are worth, how much to offer, how much to counteroffer, and so on.

Moreover, the agent will understand details that may be lost on you. For example, what if the seller counters with a **contingency**. Will you know what to do, or how to counter back? Your agent will. Is $150,000 a fair price? Your agent will have comparable home sales at his or her fingertips and will know if the answer is yes or no. A seller will probably take you more seriously if you have an agent. Without one, the seller may conclude that you are not serious about buying the home.

Put It All Together—Your agent can help you find the right home and mortgage lender, deal with getting contingencies settled, and arrange the details for the inspection and the closing.

Finding an Agent

Where do you find a good real estate professional, one who knows his or her stuff, and one whom you can trust? The best way is through satisfied customers. Referrals will tell you a lot about the professional and his or her abilities. They will also give you a good indication of whether or not you should consider doing business with a particular agent. So, if you know someone (or know someone who knows someone) who has recently bought or sold a home, find out if he or she was pleased with the broker or agent.

✓ ──────────────────────────────▶ **Ask your referrer**

☐ **Did the agent get good results?** Did the home sell near the asking price, or did your friends find the home they wanted at a price they liked? Results are what count.

☐ **Was the agent accessible?** Many real estate professionals are busy and hard to reach. A call should be returned within one day. That is what you should insist upon.

☐ **Who does the work?** A broker may delegate your work to an agent whom you don't know. You want to make sure that the person you hire is the one doing the work when it counts.

Aside from a referral from a friend or business associate, there are other ways to find a good agent:

■ **Get a recommendation from your state or local real estate board.** Realtors® are listed by area of specialty, and the board can give you the names of some of its members who are well respected in your area.

■ **Get a recommendation from other real estate professionals.** Other professionals involved in real estate transactions, including title officers, escrow officers, loan agents, and insurance professionals, can be valuable resources for referrals.

fast fact

To become a real estate agent, would-be agents must take and pass a comprehensive real estate course and then pass a state exam.

- **Check out the Internet.** Home buying has definitely gone virtual. Not only can you get interactive tours of homes online, but you can also find an agent there, too. There are many directories that list agents, and many agents have their own Web sites.
- **Look in the telephone book and the newspaper.** Many professionals advertise. Find a few ads that strike your fancy and set up a few meetings. Don't forget about the real estate section of your local newspaper. Both listing and buyer's agents advertise there. The ads generally market a specific home, but they are also a good source of attracting buyers in general.

When you call in response to a real estate ad for a specific property, the agent will ask you to come look at the advertised home. If you hit it off with the agent, he or she will probably offer to show you other similar homes in the neighborhood. Most real estate buyers find their agent by calling around, meeting a few, and finding one they like.

Interviewing the Agent

Obviously, you want a knowledgeable agent. He or she should be experienced. As with any professional, your agent should be courteous, smart, and resourceful and should return calls within twenty-four hours. Find someone whom you like. Find a go-getter! Find someone who is busy (a good sign), but not too busy to be responsive.

Attributes to look for:

- **Friendly.** Buying and selling homes is a people business, and your agent must work hand-in-hand with you, the sellers, other agents, and a variety of other people involved in the process. You want someone who is good with people and can actively represent your interests.

- **Understanding.** Look for an agent who will listen to what you want and not push his or her own agenda on you. Some agents receive a commission for steering buyers toward properties handled by their broker.
- **Knowledgeable.** You need someone who knows home buying and selling, who knows the area, and who understands the real estate contract.

Interviewing an Agent

When you meet a prospective agent, there are some questions you may want to ask. Remember, this is someone who will be helping you with a major financial decision. Ask all the questions you need to satisfy yourself that this is the right person for you.

How long have you been in business? You want someone with enough experience to thoroughly understand the home buying process. Buying a home is a complicated transaction, so the agent should have the knowledge and experience to skillfully represent your interests.

Is this your full-time occupation? You want someone who is committed full-time to the profession so he or she can maintain up-to-date knowledge.

How busy are you? Find out if the agent has the time available to represent your interests. Find out how many other buyers and/or sellers they represent.

Will you have any conflicts of interest? Find out up front if there are any potential conflicts of interest, such as would be the case if the agent also represents sellers. Make sure the agent will represent *your* interests.

What services do you offer? Find out exactly how the agent will assist you in the home buying process. What parts of searching, negotiating, financing, and purchasing your home will he or she manage? Will he or she also refer other professionals, such as a home inspector?

What fees do you charge? Understand what the agent's services will cost, who will pay for them, and exactly what you will get in return.

How do you maintain your knowledge of the home buying process? Look for someone who is committed to continuing education and/or achieving professional designations.

fast fact

When you respond to a real estate ad in the newspaper or a listing on the Internet, you are most likely calling a listing agent (that is, a seller's agent).

Find out what the agent plans to do for you, beyond just identifying and showing you homes. Will they refer you to home inspectors or lawyers, for example.

How well do you know the area? This is important for two reasons. First, it means the agent will know which homes have been on the market for a long time and which are new. Homes that haven't sold in a reasonable amount of time may have been priced too high originally, or may have some other problem that the agent should know about. The agent's knowledge will save you time by not having you look at homes that won't work for you.

Second, an established agent will know the other agents in the area, and there is a good chance he or she will know the listing agent. Therefore, your agent should know the best way to work with the listing agent and how to make the deal happen. Again, real estate is a people business, so having an agent who knows the players can only help.

How well do you know the community? Look for someone who knows the neighborhood well because you are not just buying a house; you are buying a *home* that is in a *neighborhood* that is in a *community*. The agent must have a good knowledge of all three.

When you meet with the agent, he or she should be curious about you and your housing needs. The agent should want to learn as much as possible about you so he or she can help you find and purchase a home that is right for you. If the agent doesn't seem interested in doing what is right for you, you should keep looking.

Working without an Agent

You may decide you do not want or need an agent. Perhaps you are a lawyer and feel that you know enough about real estate, contracts, and negotiating so an agent would be redundant and expensive. Or you may want to be able to offer 3 percent less for the home. Maybe you just don't want one.

THE CHALLENGE

Francisco is ready to buy his first home. A recent law school graduate, he decides he doesn't need a real estate agent to help him with his purchase. So he sets off on his own. The first problem he encounters is that because he doesn't have access to the MLS (the database of listings to which real estate professionals have access), he doesn't know which homes are available in his price range. He finds that there are only a few homes that meet his criteria advertised for sale in the paper every week.

Although it took some time, Francisco finally finds a home he likes. The owner has a listing agent so, when Francisco offers 3 percent less, to account for his lack of a buyer's agent, the owner refuses to accept less than his original price. "I know what my home is worth and what I should get, whether or not you have an agent," states the seller. Francisco is shocked and disappointed.

THE PLAN

Francisco talks about his problem with his friend Greg, who is a real estate agent. Greg suggests that perhaps Francisco started his home search on the wrong foot. He explains that a good real estate agent should be an asset in the home buying process and can help Francisco find the right home for his needs. Francisco agrees that his first attempt didn't turn out well and hires Greg. The first thing Greg does is to sit down with his friend to see what he wants and how much he can afford to spend. Greg discovers that Francisco had miscalculated the amount of home he can afford and, more importantly, that because he is a first-time home-buyer, Francisco can qualify for an FHA loan. This means Francisco can afford a nicer home than the one he was looking at, because the down payment required would be smaller.

Greg searches the MLS and finds seven homes that fit Francisco's new criteria. Francisco looks at all the houses and decides that the second home Greg shows him is the one he likes. Greg puts an offer together and presents it to the seller. The seller replies with a counteroffer for only $5,000 more, and a deal is struck. Sixty days later, Francisco owns his beautiful new home.

fast fact

A buyer's agent is hired by you and represents your (the home-buyer's) interests in finding and purchasing a home.

Or maybe you can't use an agent for the house you want. When a seller sells a home without an agent, it is called For Sale by Owner, shortened to FSBO (commonly pronounced "fizzbo"). When homeowners decide to sell a home FSBO, they are trying to save some money; they don't want to pay an agent 3 percent of what they get. You can bet also that they would rather not pay the buyer's agent 3 percent either.

You will know whether a FSBO is open to working with a buyer's agent because the ad or the brochure for the home will say something like "courtesy given to agents" or "cooperating with agents." This means that the owner knows the best way to get a buyer's agent to show their home is by offering a commission.

If you don't see that language, then it is likely the owner doesn't want to pay any commission at all, so you need to enter into the transaction on your own. Whatever the case, if you are going to go it alone, a few words of caution are in order.

Learn about Real Estate Transactions—Books are helpful, but you should also find specific information about how to execute your own home purchase. Buying a home is a complex, expensive transaction. You simply cannot go into it without having some level of knowledge and expertise.

Learn about Real Estate Contracts—Each state has its own standard real estate offer or contract. All real estate contracts are generally similar, but each state's is specific to that state, utilizing that state's laws. You need to get a copy of that contract and understand it. Often, contracts contain "magic words," which, if you don't know what they mean, can result in some nasty surprises. They can have far-reaching effects even if you know what they mean.

For instance, a standard sentence in some contracts is something called a "hold harmless" clause. While it might sound harmless enough, the clause means that you agree the other party is not responsible if something goes wrong! So you better know what the contract says, and more important, what it means, because you will be bound by it.

Learn about Negotiations—We negotiate more often than we may think. Whether asking for a raise or talking to a spouse about plans for Saturday, negotiating is a part of life. Great negotiators get what they want more often than the rest of us. So it is smart to brush up on negotiating tactics.

Remember: If you get to the stage where you are negotiating over terms, you have become a valuable commodity to the seller. Finding qualified buyers is not simple. You may be in a position of power when negotiating a purchase, and often you can ask the seller for reasonable concessions and changes.

But make sure you do your homework first. Find out how much similar homes in the area have sold for in recent sales. Are homes on the market a long time? (If so, you may be able to negotiate a great deal because the buyer needs you.) If the home is vacant, find out for how long (for you, longer could be better). The more you know, the better equipped you will be to negotiate a good deal.

Once you are presented with the counteroffer, read it carefully and then give it to your lawyer to review. If you find some part of the deal you or your lawyer doesn't like, negotiate that point. Keep in mind that although you might be presented with a preprinted counteroffer and it might seem difficult to change, it is only a contract, and the essence of contract law is that both sides must agree to all conditions. That, in fact, is why a contract is also called an agreement. You must agree. If you don't like something, you can ask to have it changed.

You certainly can buy a home by yourself, but we recommend that you consider the value a real estate professional brings to the table. After all, you want to get the home you want and the terms that are right for you.

smart step

Never sign a contract until you have read and fully understand and agree to all the terms.

fast fact

A real-estate agent systematically "steering" or restricting a client's housing search to only certain racially composed neighborhoods is a form of discrimination, and is illegal.

1 Real estate professionals include brokers, agents, and Realtors®.

2 A real estate professional can help with many tasks of the home buying process, including helping you find, negotiate for, and finance a home that is right for you.

3 Finding a good real estate professional takes some time and research. Look for a seasoned professional who is not acting as a dual agent, and check out his or her references.

4 Working without a real estate professional can be like tightrope walking without a net. You may be successful, but do consider the value of professionals. They help people buy and sell homes every day and understand the home buying process.

5 When deciding upon a real estate professional, select one who will represent *your* interests.

5 [SO MANY CHOICES:
Picking the Perfect Place]

"Be it ever so humble, there is no place like home."
—J. Howard Payne

On average, homebuyers see about fifteen homes before making a decision.

Now the fun begins. Finding the perfect place to call home should be a great adventure. Sure, it will take time and energy, and, yes, it can be stressful, but don't lose track of the fact that it is also an exciting journey. Armed with knowledge of what you can afford and where you want to look, and accompanied by a good real estate professional, you are now ready to set out to find the perfect home.

Perhaps you might have a good idea of what you are looking for—say, a Spanish-style house built in the '20s or an ultramodern town home—we recommend that you keep an open mind. There are so many home choices available that excluding whole categories may be a mistake. So in this chapter, we want to explore some of the many options you have and review some of the choices you will have to make when looking at each option.

Getting Started

Your agent will enter your search criteria into the MLS database and come up with a list of homes for you to look over. Expect to spend a lot of time with the agent the first time you go out, possibly even a whole day; he or she will need that much time to get a better idea of what you like and dislike and what you want and need.

As you look at homes, there are plenty of things to consider. Whether you are looking for a new or a used home, a condominium, a town home, or something else altogether, it is important to establish some parameters. Remember when you considered your wants versus your needs in a home in Chapter 2? Now is when you compare the factors that are important to you with the actual homes you are considering.

The U.S. Department of Housing and Urban Development (HUD) recommends that homebuyers define exactly what it is they are looking for in a home to narrow their search.

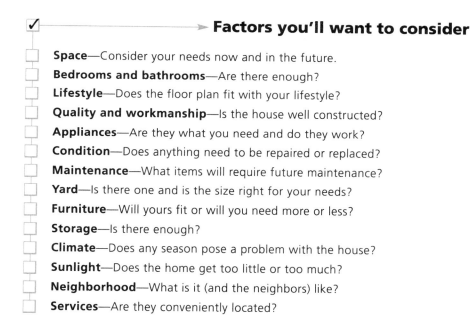

Factors you'll want to consider

- [ ] **Space**—Consider your needs now and in the future.
- [ ] **Bedrooms and bathrooms**—Are there enough?
- [ ] **Lifestyle**—Does the floor plan fit with your lifestyle?
- [ ] **Quality and workmanship**—Is the house well constructed?
- [ ] **Appliances**—Are they what you need and do they work?
- [ ] **Condition**—Does anything need to be repaired or replaced?
- [ ] **Maintenance**—What items will require future maintenance?
- [ ] **Yard**—Is there one and is the size right for your needs?
- [ ] **Furniture**—Will yours fit or will you need more or less?
- [ ] **Storage**—Is there enough?
- [ ] **Climate**—Does any season pose a problem with the house?
- [ ] **Sunlight**—Does the home get too little or too much?
- [ ] **Neighborhood**—What is it (and the neighbors) like?
- [ ] **Services**—Are they conveniently located?

The U.S. Department of Housing and Urban Development (HUD) is a government agency whose mission is a decent, safe, sanitary, and suitable living environment for every American.

Make sure the home has all the features you need. If a home you look at does not, keep looking. If you take your time and are persistent, you will probably be able to locate the home that is right for you.

You will likely see many homes, especially at the beginning of your search. It is sometimes difficult to remember each house, and the specific thing you liked or disliked about each. It is a good idea to keep accurate notes about each house you see. The information on the following worksheet can be used to keep track of the homes you see, but you may need to add specific features to it if those features are important to you.

smart step

Start Now!

Print a copy
of the home
evaluation form.

Log on to
hrblock.com/advisor

HOME EVALUATION FORM

Home address: _____

Home description: _____

Age of home: _____

Floor plan description: _____

Bedrooms (#) _____ **Bathrooms (#)** _____ **Square footage:** _____

Kitchen: Gas _____ Electric _____ Age of appliances: _____

  Distinguishing features: _____

Master bedroom: No. of closets: _____ Bathroom? _____

  Distinguishing features: _____

Bedroom two: No. of closets: _____ Bathroom? _____

  Distinguishing features: _____

Bedroom three: No. of closets: _____ Bathroom? _____

  Distinguishing features: _____

Living room: Description: _____

Dining room: Description: _____

Den: Description: _____

Other rooms: Description: _____

Custom features: _____

_____

Basement: Description: _____

Storage? _____

Heating: _____ **Air-conditioning:** _____

Electrical: _____ **Plumbing:** _____

  Age of systems: _____

Repairs required: Yes _____ No _____ If yes, what: _____

_____

Ongoing required maintenance: _____

Yard: Description: _____

Outdoor amenities: Description: _____

Homeowners' association: _____ **Dues:** _____

Neighbors: Description: _____

Neighborhood: Description: _____

Schools: _____

Support services: _____

Miscellaneous comments: _____

_____

Overall rating: Good: _____ Average: _____ Poor: _____

The New Home

New homes are great because they are equipped with many modern amenities and are designed with today's families in mind. A house built one hundred years ago may be charming, but the tiny bedrooms and kitchens from that time can become annoying quickly. Older homes have had a reputation for being sturdier and better built than newer homes, but that is not always the case these days.

Many of the modern improvements are hard to see because they are "behind the walls." Older homes can be cold, drafty, moldy, or stuffy, but not so with *well-constructed* modern homes. Modern layouts provide open floor plans, and modern insulation, heating, cooling, and ventilation systems create just the right atmosphere.

Another advantage of a new home is that you know what you are getting. Just as there is always a little seed of doubt when you buy a used car, so, too, there is a risk when buying a used home. Yes, you will have it inspected, but even so, you can never know the home's whole history. With a new home, you know when it was built and who built it. You also get what you want. Instead of being stuck with that groovy '70s avocado carpet and orange kitchen, you can pick the color schemes you want. Today's homebuilders offer a variety of options and upgrades, so you can make the house fit your personality and tastes.

Another benefit of a new home is that you know the builder. If you buy from a builder with a stellar reputation in the community, you can be fairly confident that your home will likely be well built and trouble-free.

You must learn about the builder's qualifications. How long has the company been around? Has the builder been involved in other projects? Get some references. Does the builder offer a warranty, and if so, what does it cover? Has the

smart step

Take along a camera and snap photographs of homes you look at to help you remember what features you liked best.

builder been involved in any construction defect litigation? Find out. It's important. To be sure, you should thoroughly check out the builder.

smart step

Get a copy of the builder's warranty and review it before you agree to buy a new home. Be sure you understand what it covers and for how long.

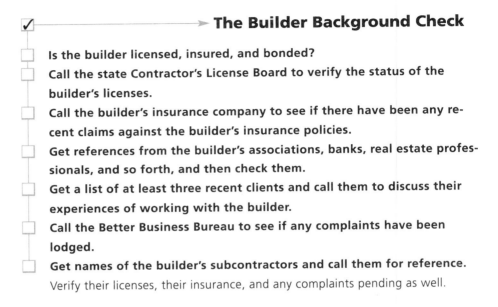

The Builder Background Check

- Is the builder licensed, insured, and bonded?
- Call the state Contractor's License Board to verify the status of the builder's licenses.
- Call the builder's insurance company to see if there have been any recent claims against the builder's insurance policies.
- Get references from the builder's associations, banks, real estate professionals, and so forth, and then check them.
- Get a list of at least three recent clients and call them to discuss their experiences of working with the builder.
- Call the Better Business Bureau to see if any complaints have been lodged.
- Get names of the builder's subcontractors and call them for reference. Verify their licenses, their insurance, and any complaints pending as well.

There are other benefits of buying a new home, including:

- **You get a warranty.** A home warranty is like an insurance policy: if something goes wrong within a specified period of time (a year, for example), the warranty covers the cost of fixing the problem. In addition, most builders will come back during that time period to fix or finish items that may have gone unnoticed when you moved in. To be fair, some pre-owned homes may also offer a warranty of some kind or you may be able to negotiate for one during contract negotiations.

- **The community is planned.** Buying a new home in a designed community means that you get the latest in neighborhood planning. Builders today try to incorporate a sense of community in their designs. Trails, bike paths, porches, and playgrounds all foster a sense of neighborliness.

■ **Control.** If you buy a new home, you will get more, if not all, of what you want in the home. The carpet will be the color you pick, the tile will be what you like, and the paint will be the color you like best. That's hard to beat.

There are also some negatives to buying a new home. First, while you can certainly have the wallpaper, carpet, and tile of your choice, anything other than the basics will probably cost more. You will also have to put additional time and money into items such as curtains, drapes, and landscaping. If big oak trees in the yard are important to you, a pre-owned home in an established neighborhood may be a better choice.

Next, not all new homes are created equal. Some are built well and others are not. Carefully consider, therefore, as mentioned before, the reputation of the builder. A new developer may create great homes in a great area, or he or she may go bust. *Caveat emptor*—let the buyer beware.

Remember that the builder's model home will be the best of the best. Builders pay top interior designers to create the perfect home, and to them, one attribute of the perfect home is that it sells. So the purpose of that gorgeous model home is to get you to buy one (almost) like it. That model home will generally be in picture-perfect condition, something most real homes are not. Also be sure to check out a model home thoroughly and consider whether or not it or a home like it will meet your needs.

Finally, learn as much about the plans for the area as possible. If the city is planning to extend Highway 99 past your subdivision in the next few years, you should know about it before you buy. Talk to the developer and/or builder, and to be extra sure, speak with someone at city hall.

smart step

You can learn more about your rights as a homebuyer by visiting HUD online at www.hud.gov

smart step

Consider the climate when selecting a home. In colder climates you may want a home that receives more sunlight, and in warmer climates you may want one that receives less.

The Older Home

Older homes are essentially the opposite of newer homes. Whereas a new home can be custom-designed, energy-efficient, and maybe a tad sterile, an older home may offer charm and character, but may require more upkeep, and may need repairs sooner. Whatever the case, the benefits of an older home are not insignificant:

- **Reputation.** In a new subdivision, it is hard to tell which location will end up being the better location. But with an older home, you will know immediately whether you are buying in a great, well-liked neighborhood or not. Schools are well established, and you will be able to determine whether or not a particular school is one to which you want to send your children. New neighborhoods don't have that sort of track record. If you can buy a house in a neighborhood with a good reputation, even a house that is not the pick of the litter, it should appreciate along with the rest of the neighborhood, if you put some time and effort into maintaining and improving it.
- **Ambience.** Crown moldings, archways, solid wood doors, lush gardens, and stone pathways are the sorts of things that give older homes the charm that so many people like. The trees aren't scrawny, as they tend to be in new subdivisions, but may be more established or mature. That is worth a lot to some homebuyers.
- **Value.** Construction costs and the psychology of buying new can mean that a new home might be quite expensive. Older homes, like used cars, may be less expensive but no less valuable. Remember, older doesn't necessarily mean ancient or decrepit; it may simply mean pre-owned.

The risk of buying a pre-owned home is that the home will require more upkeep than you want to allot to it. The possibility of necessary repairs is real and must be taken into account. Other potential issues when considering older homes are:

- **Cost of remodeling.** Remodeling a home to get it exactly the way you want it can take a lot of time and money. Totally remodeling the kitchen to add that island, granite or concrete countertops, and stainless steel refrigerator you want can easily run into the tens of thousands of dollars.
- **Cost of repairs.** Repairing or replacing antiquated or obsolete systems can be expensive. If the plumbing fails, the whole house may need to be re-plumbed to meet current building codes. If an electrical circuit goes on the fritz, a new circuit breaker box or wiring may be required.
- **Size.** Homes built years ago may have been built with a different lifestyle in mind. The bedrooms, closets, kitchen, or bathrooms may be too small or there may not be enough of them. For that matter, the whole house may be too small, or it may not fit with your lifestyle.
- **Lack of privacy.** Many older homes (and some new ones, too) were built on very small lots. Hearing your neighbor's shower run may mean your neighbor is a bit too close for comfort.

Owning an older home can be an attractive choice, but it is not for everyone. If you are not handy, or you don't want to devote the time and money to repairs and up-keep, or you simply want to buy new, a pre-owned home may not be for you.

smart step

Some older homes may contain environ-mental hazards such as asbestos or lead paint that may require professional removal before any remodeling can begin.

Condominiums, Town Homes, and Cooperatives

Condominiums, town homes, and cooperatives (co-ops) can be attractive options, especially if you are a first-time homebuyer. Many first-time buyers have less money to spend on a home and need smaller monthly payments. Because condominiums, town homes, and co-ops are often less expensive than single-family homes, they can be a great way to get started. It is important to know that there are some definite factors that you need to consider before choosing one of these options, so tread carefully.

THE CHALLENGE

Mara and Jeremy rented an apartment after they were married, but after their children were born, the space became too small for their family. The children are ready to enter school (they are ages four and five), and Mara and Jeremy want to find a home before school starts in the fall. They don't want the children to move from school to school like they did while they were growing up. The family wants to put down roots. They want to find the right home, move in, and stay there at least until the children are in middle school.

One day while driving around, they discover a new development in their area. It seems to have everything they want. They like the idea of getting a new home that has a modern kitchen, an open floor plan, and a wonderful great room. Unfortunately, all the homes in the development seem to have tiny backyards as well. They continue their search. After driving around some more in another part of town, they spot a beautiful older home in a charming neighborhood that Mara likes. The home has smaller, cozier rooms, but it also has a big backyard with huge trees and mature landscaping. The couple is torn between the appeal of a brand new home and the necessity of having adequate space for the children to play.

THE PLAN

The couple decides to interview people in the area to get a better understanding of the two neighborhoods they are considering. They start the process by taking walks in the new subdivision and talking to the people who live there. They meet plenty of families, but not many of them have children who are near the ages of the couples' own children. Everyone seems to like the development, but no one has lived in the subdivision long enough to form an opinion about the schools. The couple decides the neighborhood feels too new.

In the older neighborhood, the neighbors are a little older, and the couple finds more families with children closer in age to their own. The schools are known to be good because they have been around for fifty years and have a great reputation. The homes in the area are neatly kept and seem to have increased in value fairly predictably.

Mara and Jeremy sit down and have an honest discussion about their wants and needs. There are things they want, like a new home with an open floor plan, but they find that what they need is a quality home with good schools for their children to attend and a place with plenty of space for the children to play. They soon discover that their wants and needs are not exactly the same thing.

In the end, Mara and Jeremy opt for the older home in the older neighborhood. They like the idea of making an investment in an established neighborhood that should be a great place for their children to grow up. "It was a tough decision," said Mara, "but in the end we decided what was really important to us and made the right decision."

Let's first begin by examining the differences between these three options:

Condominiums—If you buy a condo, you are buying a unit in a group-owned building. You get a **deed** for that unit, you will probably have a mortgage (unless you pay cash), you pay property taxes, and you pay a homeowners' association fee to cover maintenance of the common areas. A board of directors governs the complex. The most important thing to understand about condos is that when you buy a condo, you only own the *interior* of the unit. The actual physical structure, the land underneath the building, the pool, the tennis courts, and other common areas including some on the inside such as stairs and hallways are owned jointly with your fellow condominium owners.

Another important thing to consider with a condominium is its resale value. There is little you can do to improve a condo's resale value because there is almost nothing you can do as an individual owner to enhance its curb appeal. When you own a single-family home, a fresh coat of paint and a little landscaping can go a long way to increasing your asking price. Not so with a condominium.

Some owners find it difficult to resell their unit for what they feel is a fair price because their pre-owned condominium often competes against new condominiums for the same buyers. If you had the choice between new and used, and the price wasn't all that much different, which would you choose? And what happens when condominium owners can't sell their units? They may try to rent the units. Given that one reason people buy condominiums is that the monthly mortgage is similar to a rent payment, finding renters may not always be that easy. Additionally, you might not enjoy living in a place with a high rate of turnover in residents as renters or short-term residents may not have the same vested interest in their units as you do.

Town Homes—When you buy a town home, you are also buying the structure and the land underneath it. Like condominium owners, owners of town homes

plain talk

A deed is the legal document that states you are the owner of the property.

Covenants,
Conditions, and
Restrictions
(CC&Rs) deter-
mine what is,
and is not,
acceptable in
a development.

generally belong to a homeowners' association. They pay monthly or annual fees for the maintenance of the exterior (condominiums include interior areas, too) common areas. If the town home has a small backyard, the owner is generally responsible for its maintenance and upkeep.

Cooperatives—A co-op is a building owned by a corporation. When you buy a co-op, what you are buying is stock in that corporation, and an exclusive, renewable lease to occupy your home for up to fifty years (generally). A board of directors governs the co-op, and your mortgage, taxes, and fees are paid according to the percentage share of your unit vis-à-vis the entire building. When looking at a co-op, bear in mind that the rules for selling or renting a co-op are generally more restrictive than the rules that govern renting a condominium. Renting out a co-op may require board approval as well.

Condo, Town Home, and Co-op Checklist

Here's a checklist of steps to take and questions to ask when considering a condominium, town home, or cooperative:

Speak with other owners in the complex. Do they like it? Why or why not?

Check out the facilities and common areas. Are they up–to-date and well kept?

Get a copy of the bylaws and review the Covenants, Conditions, and Restrictions (CC&Rs).

What is the vacancy rate?

Are there more renters or owners in the complex?

How much are the monthly association fees? What exactly do they cover? How often have they been increased and by how much?

Does the association have an adequate reserve fund established to offset future major repairs? If not, an assessment (a special charge) could be charged to all owners.

Has the homeowners' association been involved in any litigation? If so, what was the nature of the case and the outcome?

Condominiums are more common than town homes and co-ops, but each of these options presents an opportunity at home ownership. Each has features you need to carefully consider before buying, but one might be the right fit for you depending upon your needs.

A Word about Homeowners' Associations

All types of homes may or may not include membership in a homeowners' association. The amount of control an association can exert over what you do to your home, such as choosing paint colors, and what you can do with your home, such as parking a trailer in the driveway overnight, can vary significantly. Homeowners' fees are over and above your mortgage payment and may be collected on a monthly or annual basis. They can and usually do rise every year, because the common areas can be expensive to maintain. If something significant needs repair, you can be charged a special fee or assessment to cover the cost. Homeowners' association fees are yet another factor that needs to be carefully considered when choosing a home, because it will have an impact on your finances.

Over the years, some homeowners' associations have earned a bad reputation for controlling their fiefdoms too strictly. But to be completely fair, not all homeowners' associations are like that, and they can help you to maintain the value of your home by enforcing the rules associated with your development. If you want restrictions placed upon your neighbors (and you, too), to avoid potential problems and eyesores, a well-run homeowners' association can help in that regard. As a check, be sure to talk to other members of the development to see how things are run and if they are satisfied before you buy.

smart step

Consider carefully before buying one of the first homes in a new subdivision. When a project is still very new, potential problems with the development may not yet be known.

Buying Multiple Units

A great option can be buying multiple units. You can live in one and rent the other(s). **Duplexes and fourplexes** offer you the opportunity to have someone else pay your mortgage. If you add to that property's potential appreciation, you can see why becoming a homeowner/landlord can be an attractive option for some people.

Another great thing about buying a small complex is that such dwellings often fall under the guidelines of the FHA, which allows you to purchase a complex by putting down 3 percent and obtaining an FHA loan.

Here's an example: Say you find a nice fourplex in a decent neighborhood. Let's further say that the complex costs $250,000. Three percent of that is $7,500, leaving a mortgage of $242,500. At 8 percent, a 30-year mortgage amounts to $1,779 per month. Depending on the rental market, it is quite possible that you could rent the other three units for $600 per month. If you did, you could live mortgage-free ($600 x 3 = $1,800 a month). Your tenants would pay your mortgage.

There are also plenty of tax benefits to being a landlord. Property taxes, mortgage interest, repairs, and other expenses related to the rental units are generally deductible.

The downside of owning a duplex or fourplex is that you will become a landlord, and with that comes all the headaches that accompany the job: late rent, repairs, evictions, and so forth. Being a landlord is not simply a matter of collecting the rent. It's a business and must be treated as one. If you are ready for that, great, but if not, this is probably not the right choice for you.

plain talk

Duplexes and fourplexes are examples of attached (sharing a common structure), multi-family homes. Two families live in a duplex and four families live in a fourplex.

Finding the right home is a time-consuming and thought-provoking process. You must weigh the pros and cons of all your options carefully before deciding upon the type of home that best suits your needs and lifestyle. Putting in the needed effort and taking the necessary time will help you to get the home that is right for you.

the ESSENTIALS

1 Take detailed notes about each home you see so you can later remember what you have seen and make accurate comparisons among homes.

2 New homes have modern amenities that are not always present in older homes, but sometimes they lack the charm of an older home or neighborhood.

3 A new home does not necessarily mean a well-constructed home. Thoroughly check out any potential home for quality and craftsmanship.

4 Your home may not end up being a house at all. Be sure to consider all your home buying options including condominiums, town homes, and cooperatives.

5 Buying an investment property where you live in one unit and rent the other(s) can make money for you as well as giving you a home.

6 [YOU HAVE OPTIONS:
The Unconventional Purchase]

"Necessity is the mother of invention."

—Anonymous

smart step

Start Now!

Calculate the
financial value
of owning a home
versus renting.

Log on to
hrblock.com/advisor

To buy a home the conventional way, you must have good credit and money in the bank. Without both, getting into a home can be difficult, and it's quite possible that neither the owner nor the lender will take you seriously. What can you do if you have bad credit or you haven't saved enough for a down payment? In this chapter, we'll discuss a few options you may consider if your financial situation is something other than conventional.

The Unconventional Buyer

Credit problems used to mean that finding a home and obtaining a mortgage were probably out of the question. That is simply not true today. While it is certainly possible to buy a home, even with bad credit, two more things are equally true: You will probably have to look harder, and it will most likely cost you more.

If you are an unconventional buyer, you will have to be more creative. Being a financially challenged homebuyer means that you cannot simply call up a real estate agent, drive around, find a home you like, and make an offer. You will probably have to find someone who is willing to work with you and your situation.

How do you overcome these problems? Here's the secret: Find an owner who is as motivated to sell as you are to buy. You are looking for someone who needs to get out of a mortgage quickly or someone whose home has been on the market for an extended period of time.

The Unconventional Home

The unconventional home is one that has not sold and is still looking for a new owner for some reason or another. It could be that there is something seriously wrong with it physically; perhaps it is dilapidated or in need of major repairs. Maybe the home is in a poor location on a noisy, busy street, or maybe the schools nearby aren't that good. Perhaps it has an odd floor plan, a small backyard, or only one bathroom. Finally, it could just be that you are shopping in a slow real estate market and nothing is moving. Whatever the case, your job is to find that unconventional home, because an unconventional home usually also comes with a motivated seller. And a motivated seller can be a creative seller, and that's what you need.

Where do you find these unconventional homes? Here are a few ideas:

The Empty Home—If you are an unconventional buyer, one of the best things you can find is an empty home for sale. Look for an empty home that is costing someone a lot of money. It signifies that the owner has probably tried to sell it, couldn't, has moved, is now paying two mortgages, and *needs* to sell the home. It might also be a home that is now owned by a company that has taken over the home after relocating an employee. Companies generally don't want to own vacant homes for long. Either way, an empty home can be an unconventional buyer's best friend.

The Divorce Sale—These homes can be harder to find, but they are equally attractive to the unconventional buyer. A divorce often means that the parties need to sell the home quickly. If you can locate one of these homes, a creative offer can sometimes work to your advantage.

The Estate Sale—When a person dies and leaves a home to his or her heirs, the heirs will often put that home up for sale. This is another possibility for an unconventional purchase because the home may need extensive remodeling, the heirs may not agree on how to proceed, or they may not want to own a home that is located in a city or part of the country different from their own. And the rule for the unconventional buyer is: A Seller in Need Is Your Friend Indeed. If you are willing to take the home "as is," you may be able to get the heirs to sell it to you to save themselves additional headaches.

smart step

Look for estate homes for sale by looking for classified ads or signs advertising "estate sales."

smart step

Before entering into a land sales contract, a buyer should obtain a title report on the property. This report will disclose who owns the land, and whether there are any mortgages, liens, or judgments against the property.

The Newspaper Ad or Sign—The magic words you are looking for here are "owner will carry the papers" or "owner financing available." This means that the owner is willing to finance all or part of the sale. You may not need to work with a lender in this case. This option is discussed in detail later in this chapter.

The Home Headed for Foreclosure—If a home is on the verge of foreclosure, the owner might be very agreeable to a creative financing deal. Rather than have a foreclosure on their credit records, many owners in this situation are willing to sell the homes, even to needy buyers. They are needy sellers. Foreclosure notices can be found in the real estate section of the classified ads and in legal newspapers.

Unconventional Purchasing

The second issue you will face when buying a home creatively is that it will cost you more. These days, a "normal" homebuyer with good credit can usually negotiate the sales price and then get a conventional mortgage with good terms. But the person with poor credit will have very little, if any, room to negotiate the price and may have to pay a higher interest rate. That's the price you will have to pay to a homeowner who is willing to work with your special circumstances.

So once you find that needy, creative seller, what can you offer him or her? There are many ways to structure a creative home sale. For the remainder of this chapter, we will outline some of the options. Different options will work in different circumstances and with different sellers. Knowing these options will give you an assortment from which to choose.

The Installment Land Sales Contract

nstallment land sales contracts allow you to buy property over time. Rather than coming up with a big down payment, getting a loan to pay the seller, and then getting title to the home, buying with an installment land sales contract allows the seller to act as the lender. The catch is that the seller keeps the title to the property until the contract is paid in full. The property acts as collateral for the **secured debt**

The good news about an installment land sales contract is that it allows for the immediate possession of the property by the buyer. The bad news is that you don't get the title until payment of the purchase price is received in full. Remember that when you buy a home the conventional way, you get title to the property immediately upon closing.

Typically, the buyer makes monthly payments of both principal and interest. In that, the loan associated with a land sales contract is much like a mortgage. Also like a mortgage, if you default, the seller has the right to terminate the contract, retake possession of the home, and keep all payments received.

Not surprisingly, installment land sales contracts are one of the preferred options for sellers because of the aforementioned forfeiture provision, which, in the case of a default, allows the immediate recovery of the property without having to go to court. Sellers have to be concerned about the possibility of default when they enter into creative selling agreements because the buyers usually have some sort of financial challenge.

You need to be extremely careful about entering into an installment land sales contract. It is understandable why you would agree to one: If you are in a situation where you can't buy a home the conventional way, then you are obviously

plain talk

A secured debt is a debt that has some sort of collateral tied to it. Home mortgages and automobile loans are examples of secured debts.

more open to almost any deal the seller offers. "At least they are willing to work with me," you might think.

But think carefully. The deal may not be worth it. Yes, you might be able to get into the home, but what if you default for some reason? What if you get sick and miss work, or lose your job, or get divorced, or something else happens that negatively affects your financial situation? If you have to default, you will lose all that money because of the **liquidated damages** clause that is part of most installment land sales contracts.

Remember that if you have reached the point of negotiating contract terms, the seller probably needs you as much as you need him or her. The seller would probably sell the property under better terms, if possible. So if you are negotiating a contract, you are in a position of some power. You should bargain for terms that are favorable to you, such as not agreeing to the type of liquidated damages clause mentioned above. Perhaps you could negotiate for the installment land sales contract to say that in case of a default, the buyer gets credit and a refund of a part of all payments made. If you decide to enter into this sort of agreement, always have a lawyer review it thoroughly before you sign *anything*.

The Lease Option

The second option available in the creative-financing toolbox is the lease option. Why are you unable to qualify for a conventional home loan? One reason may be that you may not have enough money for a down payment. The lease option (also sometimes referred to as "rent-to-own") could be your answer.

First, you need to understand what an option is. In the corporate world, we hear about people who get stock options. What that means is that they are

plain talk

A liquidated damages clause is a section of the contract that defines what the remedy will be if one party defaults. In a land sales contract, it is usually defined as all payments made to date.

given the right to buy the company's stock at a set time for a set price. If the stock sells today for $30 a share, the option might say that in two years, the person has a right to buy the stock at $30 a share. If the asking price in two years is $40 a share, then the person is getting a good deal.

When you agree to lease a home with an option to buy it, you and the owner agree to a set price for the home. For example, let's say that price is $150,000. In two years, whether the market price goes up or down, you have first rights to buy that home—before anyone else—at that price.

The best part of a lease option from a buyer's perspective is that part of your monthly lease payments are set aside for your down payment. Typically, the tenant also agrees to pay above-market rent. So, for example, if rents for this home would normally be $600, you and the landlord might agree to have you pay $900, with $300 per month being applied toward the option. After two years, you would have paid $7,200 toward the down payment ($300 x 24 mos. = $7,200). However, you do not have to agree to pay extra rent. If $600 is the going rate, you can certainly negotiate to pay $600. Extra rent, however, gives you a larger down payment if you eventually purchase the home.

Within two years you must exercise your option: At that time, you need to secure a mortgage and buy the home. Getting a mortgage should be much easier now. Lenders want you to put anywhere from 3 to 10 percent down on the home, and if you elected to pay the higher rent, the $7,200 from our earlier example would equal almost 5 percent down on a $150,000 home.

But there is a catch. If you are unable, for any reason, to buy the home in the time allotted, you lose your entire down payment. That's what the seller gets for taking the home off the market for two years and giving you an exclusive right to buy it for that period of time. So if you can't get a loan, you'll forfeit the deposit.

smart step

Be sure to have the lease drawn up in such a way that you cannot easily default or otherwise forfeit your option payments. For example, if you fall behind on rent, a clause indicating that you have 45 days to fix the problem would be beneficial.

Lease options are a risk. First, you may lose your money. Second, you will probably be paying above-market rents for two years (more or less). Finally, you still may not be able to get financing when the time comes. So it is a good idea, before entering into a lease option, to meet with a mortgage lender, explain your situation, and find out what you need to do over the next two years to get approved for a loan (for example, clean up your credit, pay off some outstanding debts, etc.).

But the benefits of lease options can outweigh the risks. First, you are locking in today's price for a home that you won't be purchasing for two years. If homes appreciate in your area at 5 percent per year, today's $150,000 home will be worth about $165,000 in two years. That's a great deal. Second, if you don't have the money today for a down payment, by agreeing to a lease option, you are forced to save $7,200 over the next two years. It can be a good deal.

Owner Financing

The most common type of creative financing for the homebuyer is owner financing, also known as an "owner carryback." As the name implies, with owner financing, the seller agrees to finance all or part of the buyer's purchase, in effect acting as both seller and lender. For instance, let's say that the owner has a home worth $150,000 that he owns outright, but that he cannot sell for some reason. He might agree to sell it to you and "carry the note." That is, instead of you getting a mortgage and paying the owner off, the owner becomes the lender and sells you the home, and you pay the owner directly (instead of the lender). If you default, the owner retakes possession of the home.

Sellers may be open to this option for various reasons:

- **The debt is secured.** If the buyer defaults, the seller can always foreclose on the property.

- **The owner makes money.** Rather than the lender earning your interest, the seller gets it.
- **The owner secures a higher interest rate from the buyer.** If the going rate for a home loan is 6 percent, an owner carryback deal might pay the owner 8 percent.
- **The owner can get a higher price for the home.** Unconventional buyers are usually willing to pay the full asking price.
- **The owner saves on commissions.** No real estate agents means sellers save an additional 6 percent.
- **The agreement is often short-term.** With a typical owner-financed deal, the buyer must make a **balloon payment** and pay the seller off (usually by refinancing the entire loan with a conventional lender) within a set period of time, say, five years.

How much will the owner finance? That's the most important question to ask. Some will finance the entire purchase while others will finance only part of it, requesting that you get a mortgage for the balance. The best place to find a deal like this is in the classifieds. Look for an ad that says something like "owner will carry contract" or "owner will carry papers" or "owner financing available." But, as with any other contract, make sure you understand and agree to all the terms and have your lawyer review the contract before you sign anything.

Equity Sharing

Equity sharing is best when you have decent credit, but you don't have enough money for the down payment. If you can find a partner with enough money to make the down payment, then the two of you buy the home together. You will live in it, you will make the mortgage payments, but

plain talk

A balloon payment is a large, lump sum payment at the maturity date of the note.

THE CHALLENGE

Ellen, David, and their two children want to buy a home. Unfortunately, some financial problems a few years earlier make that dream seem impossible. The downturn in the stock market has eaten up their savings, and a previous bankruptcy and some other financial difficulties with a failed business have resulted in the couple having a low credit score. The best mortgage rate the couple can get is 10 percent. Adding to their dilemma, many sellers are reluctant to work with them because of the bankruptcy. David and Ellen feel stuck.

THE PLAN

David understands that some sellers feel desperate if their home has been on the market for a while. So he begins to scour the Sunday real-estate ads for homes that don't seem to be moving. He notices one ad that runs every other week for several months. One day, he goes to look at the home, which was advertised for $150,000. It isn't perfect: It is slightly smaller than the couple wants, and it needs some repairs, but David is handy and feels he can handle most of them.

He talks to the owner and finds out that she needs to sell the home. The owner's mother had recently passed away and left her the home. The owner lives several hundred miles away and doesn't want to keep the home or use it as a rental property because she feels the distance is too far for her to be able to maintain the home. After talking further to Ellen and David, the owner agrees to a creative option to sell them the home. The owner understands what the couple is going through because she, too, had once filed bankruptcy. She wants to see a good family live in the home where she grew up. The owner agrees to carry (owner finance) a first mortgage of $100,000 if David can get a second mortgage for $50,000.

Ellen and David talk with several lenders and discover that with the seller willing to carry a note that large, getting a loan is easier. However, every lender demands that they carry the first mortgage and that the owner carry a second. The lenders want to be paid first in case of a foreclosure, which means the previous owner would get paid second. David speaks with the owner again, and amazingly, she agrees to the terms, because she really wants to sell the home and move on with her life. David, Ellen, and the children move in a few months later and finally have a place to call home.

your partner will own a portion of it, and when you sell or refinance, he or she will get that portion of the proceeds.

In an equity share agreement (sometimes referred to as a shared equity agreement), you are called the *occupier* and your partner is called the *investor*. The occupier has the exclusive right to occupy the premises. The occupier also assumes all the rights and obligations of home ownership.

Once you agree to terms with your investor, you, the investor, or both of you obtain a mortgage for the property (depending upon your agreement). You further agree to a termination date for the equity share agreement; usually it is between three and ten years. In the interim, both you and the investor are entitled to the tax benefits of real estate ownership (you share the mortgage interest deduction, if you were both liable for the mortgage, and the property tax deduction as well).

Then, before the termination date, you either refinance or sell the property at your discretion. If you decide to refinance, you hire a professional appraiser to set the price. After a price has been set, the investor gets his or her down payment back and a portion of the gain, but you get full credit for any money you spent improving the property.

For the occupier, equity sharing is a chance to become a homeowner without having a large down payment, and without having the seller acting as your apparent landlord (as with an owner-financed deal). The arrangement is also good for the investor, who can make an excellent return on his or her investment.

An equity share can be a great way to get into a home with little or no money. To do this correctly, however, *do not* draft your own equity share agreement. Find a good real estate lawyer to make sure your interests are protected.

fast fact

Equity sharing is attractive to homebuyers in upper-end markets. A partner who can make a substantial down payment makes it easier to afford monthly payments for a nicer home.

A first mortgage will take legal priority over all others.

COMPARING UNCONVENTIONAL PURCHASE OPTIONS			
TYPE OF AGREEMENT	**OWNERSHIP STATUS**	**RISKS**	**BENEFITS**
Installment Land Sales Contract	Delayed: Buyer owns the property only at the end of the contract	High: If buyer defaults, he or she loses all his or her money	Low: No ownership until contract is fully completed
Lease Option	Delayed: Buyer owns the property only after he or she exercises the option	Medium: If buyer fails to (or can't) exercise the option, he or she loses all option money	Medium: Buyer remains a tenant until the option is exercised
Owner Financing	Immediate: Buyer owns the property once a contract is entered into	Low: Buyer usually puts little down and thus has little to lose	High: Immediate ownership with little risk
Equity Share	Immediate: Buyer owns the property once a contract is entered into	Low: Buyer usually puts little down and thus has little to lose	Medium: Ownership is split (usually 50-50)

If you are an unconventional buyer, it should be calming to know that if you are in a situation where you can't make an offer on a home and get a mortgage, you still have options. Home sellers enter into unconventional purchase agreements every day, and there is no reason why you can't be the beneficiary of one of those deals. The deals will probably cost more than a regular home purchase, but considering the alternative (no home ownership at all), it can still make sense for the right situation.

the ESSENTIALS

1. If you take the time to look, it is possible to find motivated sellers, especially in a slow market. Buying a home from a motivated seller can result in a good deal for you.

2. Installment land sales contracts are risky because if you default, you normally lose all the money you have put into the deal. As such, they should only be used as a last option.

3. Lease options can be a creative way to lock in a purchase price for a home and build up funds for a down payment.

4. Owner financing can help both a motivated buyer and a seller complete a deal by having the seller act as the lender.

5. Equity sharing works well if you have good credit but not enough money for the down payment. An occupier and an investor finance the home together. After a set amount of time, the occupier either sells the home and splits the gain, or refinances and buys the investor's share.

smart step

If you want to maintain a good credit history, pay all your bills on time.

7 [GET IT IN WRITING: The Basics of Contracts and Negotiations]

"A verbal contract isn't worth the paper it is written on."
—Samuel Goldwyn

Finding a home you love in a neighborhood you like is the first step down the path to home ownership. You also have to be able to negotiate a price you can afford, find a loan that will work for your personal financial situation, and close the deal. Sometimes buying a home goes smoothly: Everything checks out, everyone performs their roles well, inspections reveal no major problems, and documents are prepared on time. Just as often, the process gets sidetracked; for example, the buyer thought the seller was going to repair the fence before closing, or the seller thought the buyer didn't want a home warranty. Your contract is your protection. To create a contract that protects and benefits you, you must understand contracts generally and real estate contracts specifically. That is what this chapter is all about.

Contracts 101

Generally speaking, you need to meet three criteria to create a valid, legally enforceable **contract**: an offer, acceptance of that offer, and something called "consideration." Let's discuss each of these in more detail.

Offer—The first step toward creating a contract is an offer by one side that invites the other side to accept it. Legally, an offer is defined as a communication of willingness to enter into an agreement that justifies another person understanding that his or her acceptance of the agreement is invited, and that if he or she accepts, an agreement will exist.

This means an offer must be clear, unequivocal (unmistakable), and specific. If you go to a new subdivision and say to the contractor, "I want to buy a home," your statement is not a legal offer. It is too general. On the other hand, stating "I will pay you $135,000 for the home located at 36 Timothy Terrace" is an offer. It is clear and specific, and it invites a specific response. An offer for a home must always be in writing, and the process normally involves the use of a standard contract approved by your state.

Acceptance—Acceptance occurs when the offeree (the seller) makes an affirmative (positive) response to the offer. If the seller says to you, "That sounds good, but let me think about it overnight," that is not an acceptance because it is not an unequivocal response that would create an agreement. "OK, I accept your offer" is an acceptance. Note again that for a sale of real estate, the acceptance, like the offer, must be in writing. Typically, the seller signs the offer sheet submitted by the buyer.

What if the seller says to you, "How about $142,000?" That is not an acceptance. This response is a counteroffer, which puts you in the position of being the party who can accept. This offer/counteroffer dance can go on until both parties finally agree or disagree. It is usually part of a home sales negotiation and is examined in detail later in this chapter.

Consideration—Consideration means that for a contract to be created, something of legal value must be exchanged. The exchange can involve goods, services, or promises to perform. For example, if I say, "I will wash your car," and you say, "Great," a contract has not been created because there is no bargain and no exchange. The exchange is simply a promise by me. But if I say, "I will wash your car for $1," and you reply, "Great," then a contract has been created; we have bargained and exchanged something of value—my efforts for your money.

An offer, acceptance, and consideration are necessary to create any legal contract. So let's examine how they work in the context of a real estate contract.

smart step

If given a choice, you might consider making an offer on a *lesser* home in a *better* neighborhood rather than a *better* home in a *lesser* neighborhood. You can improve your home, but it is tough to improve the neighborhood.

The Real Estate Purchase Contract

If only making an offer on a home was as simple as saying "I will pay you $142,000." First, oral offers to buy real estate aren't binding for either the buyer or the seller, so your offer must be in written form. Second, the real estate purchase contract is a complex document, detailing all aspects of the deal. Most (they vary by state) are six pages or longer.

The real estate purchase contract is usually a form adopted by your state, although it may simply be a standard contract you can get from your real estate agent or lawyer. The prospective buyer fills out the form, specifying the details of the offer. The buyer gives the offer to the seller, who either signs it or makes a counteroffer. Once you both agree to all terms, you both sign it and it becomes your contract.

Before signing the contract, you must familiarize yourself with it. Far too often, buyers fail to read the contract in advance. Your agent will help you fill it out, but even so, you need to know what it says because it is going to obligate you if the seller signs it. Buyers often get excited about a home, are eager to make an offer, don't know (or care) what they are committing to in all that preprinted language, and then get stuck with all of the provisions, both good and bad. There may be something in there that you don't like, but if you haven't taken the time to read the contract and you have signed it anyway, you are going to be stuck with it, like it or not.

Ask your real estate agent or lawyer to give you a sample copy of the purchase contract. Review it with him or her. If there is something you don't understand, ask for an explanation. Decide which specific terms you want to include in the contract and which you do not. Remember: Just because a statement is preprinted on the form, you do not have to keep it in there. Some parts of the contract must remain, but others can be crossed out. It is, after all, your contract. Ask your lawyer if you aren't sure which items can be changed and which cannot.

It is important to understand that the offer sheet also serves as the basis for your contract. In fact, once the seller signs it, it *is* your contract. You must be very thorough and very specific about what the terms of the deal will be.

✓ → **The offer will need to contain the following**

☐ **Names of the buyers and sellers**

☐ **The address of the property**

☐ **The offer price**

☐ **An earnest money deposit**

☐ **Terms**—Will it be an all-cash sale? Is it contingent upon getting a mortgage? Is it contingent upon you selling your home? How much is the down payment?

☐ **The seller's promise to provide** clear title

☐ **The need for an inspection**

☐ **A projected date for closing**

☐ **A projected occupancy date**

☐ **Descriptions of who will pay the fees**

☐ **An inventory of any personal property to be included in the sale**

☐ **Disclosures of any known defects**

☐ **A limit of the length of time that the offer will be viable, usually a week or less**

☐ **Arbitration clauses**

☐ **Contingency clauses** (such as financing)

Each of these items is important, and a few are worth closer examination. Among the important clauses for you to think about are:

plain talk

Clear title means that no one else has any claims against the property. In other words, there are no judgments or other legal obstructions that would prevent the property from being transferred.

Earnest Money Deposit—Almost all real estate purchase offers include a good faith deposit of funds from the buyer to the seller. The money is deposited in **escrow** and held by the escrow company (a neutral third party or sometimes a lawyer). The deposit shows the seller that you are serious about acting in good faith to purchase the home. An earnest money deposit may be any amount and it is usually established by local custom. The amount may also serve to send a signal to the seller. From the seller's perspective, the more money the buyer places in escrow, the more serious the offer. A small deposit may indicate that you are not really committed, and the seller may therefore decide to reject your offer.

Contingencies—If your offer says something like "This offer is contingent upon (or subject to) _____," you are telling the seller that the deal will only go through *if* that event occurs. Contingencies are for your protection.

Inspection Contingency—The first contingency you should include in any offer you make is that the home will be subject to one or more professional inspections by an inspector of your choice, and that your offer is expressly contingent upon your approval of the reports. Among the inspections to consider are those for termites and other pests, those to determine boundaries, appraisals, title reviews, and a structural analysis. We will discuss inspections more fully in the next chapter because you certainly don't want to purchase a home that is full of problems.

Structural inspections are critical. Here, an inspector goes to the home to find out if there are any physical defects in the structure and what repairs are needed. It is important that the buyer attends this inspection. It is a chance to examine the home's structure and foundation, ask questions, and learn more about the condition of the home. This is your inspector, and he or she is there to help you make a good decision about the quality of the home.

plain talk

Escrow is an independent, neutral third-party process that accepts money from the buyer and the title from the seller, and exchanges them.

Financing Contingency—The real estate purchase offer should include a clause that states that any offer is expressly contingent upon you getting appropriate financing. You may be preapproved for a loan, but even so, you need this clause. The lender has yet to appraise the home and any loan you get will be contingent upon that appraisal, even if you are preapproved. So you need a financing contingency clause to prevent you from being obligated to purchase the home if you are unable to secure a loan.

Liquidated Damages—Most preprinted real estate purchase contracts include a liquidated damages clause. It states that if the buyer fails to buy the home without **good cause** after entering into the agreement, the seller is entitled to keep the buyer's earnest money deposit as damages. Most sellers require such a clause.

Personal Property—Anything that is not fixed to the property is considered the personal property of the owner (as opposed to his or her real property). Examples include drapes, patio furniture, washer and dryer, and so forth. If you want any personal property to be part of the sale, be sure to list it in the purchase offer.

Arbitration—Many real estate purchase contracts mandate arbitration in case a dispute arises. Arbitration is like an expedited trial, and the outcome is usually not open to appeal (that is, the decision is final). The problem is, arbitrators are not judges, and by forgoing the right to sue, you are giving up an important legal right: If you are unhappy for any reason with the arbitrator's decision (if he made a mistake, for instance), you may be out of luck. You can't sue and you can't appeal. Therefore, if you unfortunately end up in a dispute worth fighting over, it is better not to tie one of your arms behind your back before you start.

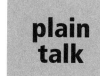

plain talk

Good cause is a legally valid reason. Backing out of a contract because you could not obtain financing is good cause, but backing out because you changed your mind is not.

Finally, it is important to understand that when it comes to real estate, oral promises are not enforceable. If the seller told you that he or she would throw in the portable hot tub with the sale and if that commitment is not in the contract, he or she doesn't have to do it. So be sure to add all promises to the offer sheet.

Making an Offer

How much should you offer? It is impossible to say because each situation is so different. You must consider the market, the needs of the seller, and how much you want the home, and then offer an amount that you can afford but which is lower than the price you think the home should ultimately command. If the seller accepts, great! If not, the seller will either counteroffer (giving you an idea about what he or she is thinking), or reject your offer altogether. If the seller rejects your offer, you can always make a second, higher offer.

Your offer should stem from having done your homework. You need to know:

- **How long the property has been on the market**
- **Why the house is being sold.** Is it a divorce or an estate sale? If so, a reduced offer may work.
- **What prices comparable (similar) homes in the area are commanding**
- **What the market is like in general.** Are homes selling quickly or slowly? Are there multiple offers on a single home or are offers hard to come by?

Knowing these details can help you figure out what the home is worth and how motivated the seller is. The law of supply and demand is what is in play here. If there are a lot of buyers who want the same home, or if the market is hot, you will probably need to offer full price to close the deal. But if the home has been on the market for an extended period of time, such as six months, you can probably safely make an offer for less than the asking price.

smart step

It may help to think of a contract as a private set of laws. Between two parties, almost anything legal, that is mutually agreeable, is permissible.

When making an offer, it is reasonable to focus on the price, but at the same time, don't lose track of the other details. The conditions and other details specified above are important and must be addressed. At the same time, you should consider items such as who pays for inspections, buyer's closing costs, real estate agent fees, and repairs. The sale price of the home is important, but remember there are many other items to consider as well.

If the seller likes your offer and signs your offer sheet (an oral acceptance is not valid), you have a binding contract. If the seller doesn't accept your offer and wants to counteroffer, he or she will accept the parts of your offer that are agreeable. Whenever a party makes a counteroffer, he or she becomes the offeror, and the other side is then free to accept or reject the offer.

Buyers and sellers may go through the several stages of offers and counteroffers before settling upon agreeable prices and terms. This brings us to the question then: How *do* you negotiate a great deal?

smart step

Make sure you understand and agree with all terms in a contract before you sign it.

Negotiating a Deal

Let's assume that you are buying a home in a normal market. Homes come up for sale, stay listed for a while, and then are sold. How do you get the best deal possible? First, realize that you could be in a strong bargaining position in relation to the seller if you are already preapproved, if you are an all-cash buyer, or if you don't have to sell your home to make this deal work. If any of these three things are present, the seller knows that you are ready to buy, now.

Also, remember that a little bluffing is generally part of the game. For example, you might explain to the seller that before making an offer, you will be looking at other homes, too. You will have the upper hand in your negotiations if the

THE CHALLENGE

Leonard believes himself to be a great negotiator and thinks he knows a lot about real estate, so he decides not to hire a real estate agent to help him search for a new home. After looking around for about six months, Leonard finally finds a home he likes. It is an older home in a quiet neighborhood that is close to his job. It has been on the market for a while, and Leonard thinks it hasn't sold because it is overpriced. The owner is asking $179,000 for the home, but Leonard concludes that it is worth only about $139,000 because of its age. Leonard thinks this is an opportunity to get a great bargain on the home, because surely the owner is desperate to sell since the home has been for sale for so long. He gets a copy of a standard real estate contract, fills it out, and offers $119,000, sure that the owner will counteroffer a little bit higher. The owner rejects the offer outright, and doesn't even give a counteroffer. Leonard calls the owner to discuss the offer and is told not to call back.

THE PLAN

Leonard wants the home, but he doesn't know how to salvage the deal. He realizes that he needs some help and calls a real estate agent he knows. The agent calls the owner and asks for more details about the home. The agent also asks if anything can be done to salvage the sale.

The owner tells the agent that he has lived in the home for twenty-five years, raised his children there, is very attached to the place, and is not in a rush to sell it. He also says that Leonard seems brash and that the low ball offer offended him. The owner feels there is no need to make a counteroffer.

The agent explains the seller's point of view to Leonard. He also explains that Leonard's $119,000 offer was way off. Although the home was 25 years old, it was well constructed and well taken care of, and $169,000 was closer to its market value. To top it off, Leonard had failed to take into account the fact that the home sat on a double lot. The agent explains that if Leonard wants the home, he must offer much more than $119,000. Leonard decides he does want the home, so he offers $159,000. The owner counteroffers and agrees to split the difference between the offer and his original asking price. Leonard ends up buying the home for $169,000.

"To be a good negotiator, I learned that you need to have all the facts first," Leonard remarked to his agent. "Next time, I'll leave it to you."

other side thinks you are willing to walk away. If you go to a car lot and look at a car, you can bargain better if the salesman truly thinks you are willing to walk away and purchase from another dealer. The same is true in a home sale. If the seller thinks you could just as easily go elsewhere, he or she will probably be more willing to negotiate.

It is smart to put yourself in the strongest negotiating position possible, but, ultimately, what you want to end up with is a win-win situation. Coming in strong simply makes sure that you get your side of that equation.

If you find a home you love, one that you are willing to take out a mortgage to get, you don't want to drive too hard a bargain or you might drive yourself right out of contention. Many home sales have fallen through because one side got sick of the other and figured out a way to kill the deal. So go in, work to get the best deal you can, but make sure the other side gets some of what they need, too. If they don't, you might lose that home.

Here are a few more important tips for negotiating a great home purchase:

Fair Offer—A lowball (ridiculously low) offer to a seller sometimes works, but it can also be perceived as an insult by the seller. You need that seller to agree to your offer, so starting out with an insult is not a good idea. Remember: The seller lives there, and the house is his or her *home*. Just as sellers shouldn't overprice their homes to start with, buyers should avoid making a lowball offer. Find out what comparable home sales are in the neighborhood and start somewhere below that point.

Quid Pro Quo—This is Latin for "what for what," or the exchange of one thing for another by agreement. Buying a home is a negotiation. You will not get everything you want and neither will the seller. If you can give the other side some of what they want, you can usually get some of what you want. For ex-

fast fact

Buyers normally want every possible problem covered by a contingency (so they can get out of the contract if there is a problem), but sellers prefer a contract that is free of contingencies.

ample, if the seller wants the full purchase price, perhaps he or she will agree to pay for more of the closing costs. The seller and the buyer must be willing to compromise. You win some, they win some, the deal closes, and you get a home you love.

You might be able to find a needy seller, one whom you can force a deal upon, but these are the deals that most often fall apart. A lot of hoops have to be jumped through to transfer real estate and keep in mind that an angry seller might make your life miserable by being difficult throughout the process.

Table It—If there is some part of the deal that you don't like and which both sides can't agree upon, table it for now. Figure out everything else and then re-visit the troublesome issue. Having everything else done should make it easier to figure out the issue that remains.

Rely on Experts—If you hired a real estate agent or a lawyer, you did so for a reason. He or she is there to help you. They are the experts, they have closed deals many times before, and their advice should usually be heeded. If you didn't hire any experts to help you and find yourself not making any progress, perhaps you should consider hiring the expertise you need.

In the end, the thing to remember is that your contract is your protection. There is an old legal saying that goes, "If you write at all, write it all, for the law as-sumes you wrote it all." What does that mean for you? It means that you need to make sure all the terms you want are in the contract and that you understand and agree to every one of them *before* signing. Once you have signed the con-tract, it will be too late to add, delete, or change any terms. By working with the seller, you should be able to get most of what you want, and the seller should be able to get most of what he or she wants, too. When that happens, a deal is struck that both sides will live up to, which is the goal.

the ESSENTIALS

1 To create a valid real estate contract, you need an offer, an acceptance, and a bargained-for exchange. All these elements must be present and in writing or the contract is not valid.

2 It is important to familiarize yourself with all aspects of the standard real estate purchase contract. Make sure you understand and agree to all the terms before you sign.

3 Making a good offer is often a matter of knowing the market. Market conditions may allow you to negotiate items such as price, loan terms, and so forth.

4 Negotiate for a win-win deal, but always consider what is in your best interests. If all parties to the deal are relatively satisfied, the deal will most likely close.

5 Consider relying on experts to guide you through the process. Your real estate agent can help you with negotiations, and your lawyer can advise you if the terms are favorable.

smart step

Do not rely on oral promises when purchasing your home. Get everything in writing to protect your interests.

8 [HOME HEALTH: Your Home's Checkup—The Home Inspection]

. . . trust, but verify.

—Russian proverb

The home you want probably looks great. Any smart homeowner who wants to sell his or her home spends time and money working on its curb appeal—that is, how it looks. Like the person trying to sell a used car, the savvy homeowner knows that how a home looks can determine whether it sells and how much he or she will receive for it.

But there is more to a home than what meets the eye. Just as you should never buy a used car without having it checked out by a mechanic, you shouldn't buy a home without having it inspected. What kind of inspection? You must insist on a very thorough inspection by a knowledgeable and experienced professional.

A **home inspection** is an unbiased look under the hood of your potential home. Does everything work right? What repairs are needed now? What repairs will probably be needed in the future? Is the home structurally sound? A home inspection can help answer these questions and more, plus provide some peace of mind before you purchase your home.

Do You Really Need a Home Inspection?

In a hot market, some buyers may think that if they forgo the inspection contingency, their offer is more likely to be accepted. They may be right, but is it worth the risk? Forgoing an inspection might help you get the home you love, but later you may see your dream home turn into a nightmare. Skipping the inspection is a huge gamble. Essentially, not getting a home inspected means that you are buying the home as is with any and all faults it may have. There are many problems that may not be obvious to the untrained eye, but a professional home inspector may be able to spot them. Occasionally, a homeowner may even attempt to hide problems to increase the chances the home will sell for the price he or she wants. Is that something you can live with?

Finding a Good Home Inspector

fast fact

The best place to find a qualified home inspector is generally through a referral. If you have a friend, business acquaintance, or family member who was satisfied with a recent home inspection, that is a good place to start. Apart from that, names of local inspectors and inspection companies can be obtained from a number of sources:

- **By contacting national accrediting organizations,** such as the American Society of Home Inspectors (ASHI) or the National Association of Home Inspectors Inc. (NAHI)
- **Your lender**
- **Your real estate agent**
- **The telephone book** (look under "Building Inspection Service" or "Home Inspection")
- **Online**
- **The Sunday real estate section of the paper**

Laws in most states require a seller to disclose to the buyer any known defects that negatively affect the value of the home.

It may not be hard to find a home inspector, but you should verify that the inspector you choose is qualified. Here are some things to consider:

Reputation and Experience—The home inspection company and/or the home inspector you select should have a reputation for quality service and thoroughness. Focus on how long both the company and inspector who will be performing your inspection have been in business, how many inspections they have performed, and if there have been any problems.

Qualifications—Find out the details of the inspector's training and background. Some inspectors are engineers, others are contractors, and still others simply understand homes and how they work. One background is not necessarily better than another. What is important is to find a home inspector with both experience and knowledge. Note, too, that depending upon the home you

smart step

Contact the National Lead Information Center at 800-424-LEAD (5323) for more information about lead hazards.

are looking at, you may also need someone who is an expert with environmental hazards such as asbestos or lead-based paint.

You have the option of hiring an inspector who works for a nationwide home inspection company, one who is self-employed, or one who works for a local establishment. One reason that you may want to choose a national home inspection company instead of a local home inspector is that national companies generally require ongoing training and often offer their inspectors technical support. What if the inspector runs into an unusual problem? A national company may be able to offer additional expertise to the particular inspector that a local inspector may not be able to access.

Individual inspectors may also have access to ongoing training. There is training available to teach proper home inspection, and there are professional societies and trade associations that offer ongoing training and education. Participating in ongoing professional training is a sign that your inspector is staying current in the necessary areas of residential construction and understands the home inspection process.

Interviewing an Inspector

- **Number of years in business**—You are looking for experience.
- **Initial training received**—What qualifications does the inspector have?
- **Access to ongoing training**—Is the inspector current in the field?
- **Number of inspections performed**—Does the inspector put his or her knowledge to work on a full-time basis, or does the inspector work part time?
- **Length of time to perform an inspection**—Is the inspector thorough?
- **Can you watch?**—Find an inspector who agrees to or better yet encourages you to attend the inspection. It will give you a firsthand look at the home and help you understand the report when you review it.
- **What type of report does the inspector produce**—What does the report cover and in how much detail? Ask for a sample of an actual report.

Errors & Omissions insurance—If the inspector makes a mistake or misses something, is there coverage available for your protection?

☐ **Membership in professional societies or trade associations**—Is the inspector committed to professional standards?

The Report—Ask to see a copy of a typical report issued by the inspector. At a minimum, you need to know exactly what will be inspected. A brief or cursory report with few details will be of little use. You want to see a detailed written report, not just checkmarks on a form. Your inspection report should provide you with an assessment of the home and its many systems. It should fully explain any immediate concerns, what repairs may be needed now and in the future, potential safety hazards, and the health of the major systems (plumbing, electrical, etc.) including their age.

✓ ────────────────────────────► **Ask to see**

☐ **A current report**—Find out what information the report will contain.

☐ **Level of detail**—How specific is the report's information?

☐ **Timing**—How soon after the inspection can you expect to receive the report?

Insurance—Does the company and/or inspector have liability insurance in case the inspector makes a mistake? The insurance usually takes the form of Errors & Omissions coverage and will help protect you in case something is missed.

✓ ────────────────────────────► **Find out about**

☐ **Coverage**—Is there coverage available in case something is missed or an error is made? Find out what is covered and to what extent.

☐ **Company**—The name of the insurance carrier that issued the policy. Does a reputable firm back up the coverage?

☐ **Claims**—Has the policy been used and what were the circumstances?

plain talk

Errors & Omissions insurance is a type of professional liability coverage that provides protection against claims due to errors or oversight in the performance of professional duties.

Select an inspector who *does not* perform repair work to avoid a potential conflict of interest.

References—Get the names and telephone numbers of several homeowners who have used this inspector's services so you can ask them if they were satisfied with the inspector and the inspection. Make sure you speak with people who have owned their home for a year or more because problems overlooked by an inspector may take a while to show up.

✓ ——————————————————————————————> **Ask to see**

☐ **List of references**—Obtain the names of at least three people who have used this inspector.

☐ **Contact information**—Be sure to get the addresses and phone numbers for the references.

Scope of the Inspection

A home inspection must be thorough and include both the exterior and interior of the home. It should cover every major area of the home and the many systems that are a part of it. The inspection should be an objective evaluation that provides you with an in-depth look at the home and its current condition. Here are some major areas of the home that should be looked at and some of the items that should be evaluated. Your home may not include some of the items or may have additional items.

- **Structural system** (foundation, framing, floors, walls, ceilings, roof)
- **Exterior** (wall covering, trim, decks, steps, porches, railings, eaves, vegetation, grading, drainage, retaining walls, walkways, patios, driveways)
- **Roof** (covering, drainage, skylights, flashing)
- **Plumbing** (water supply, gas supply, pipes, fixtures, faucets, drains, water heater, vents, flues, fuel storage)
- **Electrical** (main service drop, service grounding, service panels, conductors, protective devices, fixtures, switches, receptacles)

- **Heating system** (equipment, flues, chimneys)
- **Air-conditioning** (equipment)
- **Interior** (walls, ceilings, floors, steps, stairways, railings, cabinets, doors, windows, garage doors and openers)
- **Insulation and ventilation** (insulation, vapor barriers, attic and foundation ventilation, mechanical ventilation)
- **Fireplaces** (components, vents, flues, chimneys)

In certain circumstances, additional inspections or testing (sometimes at an extra cost) may be required. For example, most lenders will require a termite (pest) inspection in addition to the basic home inspection. Beyond that, you may need special inspections for items such as:

- **Hazardous materials** (such as lead, asbestos, formaldehyde, and radon)
- **Pools or spas**
- **Water quality**
- **Wells**
- **Septic tanks**
- **Buried fuel tanks**

smart step

Be sure your inspector examines the home's chimney. A poorly maintained chimney can be a fire hazard.

Common Problems

Home inspections usually come up with something interesting or something you didn't know about the home you want to purchase. Sometimes these things are deal-breakers and other times not, but that is why you should have the home inspected. Identifying defects before you purchase the home can mean a reduced selling price, having the seller pay for the cost of the repairs, or even walking away from the home if the problems are serious.

What are some of the problems that might show up on your inspection report? From the catastrophic to the common, here are some items looked at and discovered during home inspections:

Structural Problems—Cracks in the foundation may indicate a structural issue resulting from poor design, poor construction, settling, or water damage. Damage from insects such as termites and carpenter bees or damage from dry rot can be expensive to repair.

Exterior Problems—Siding, windows, and doors may exhibit deterioration including chipped or failing paint, or inadequate or failing weather-stripping or caulking. These can lead to water and air intrusion in the home.

Interior Problems—A wet basement can be a sign of water intrusion, which can cause stains, mold, mildew, odor, and so forth. Paint surfaces on homes constructed prior to 1978 may contain lead, and those homes built before 1960 probably do contain lead, unless it has been removed.

Roof Problems—Many homes have older or damaged roofs, and problems often include deterioration of the roofing material (such as broken or missing shingles or tile) or defective flashing, both of which may allow water intrusion into the home.

Plumbing Problems—Outdated plumbing, pipe deterioration, poor or incompatible piping materials, and leaks may be found. Fixtures, faucets, bathtubs, and showers may leak.

Electrical Problems—The electrical system may be outdated or may be the wrong size for the home. The service panel or the wiring may need to be replaced. Many homes wired in the 1960s and '70s have aluminum wiring, and if so, the inspector should determine if a retrofit has been installed. If the home is very old, it may have knob and tube wiring, which can be hazardous and expensive to replace. There may not be enough electrical outlets in the home and non-professional installations or repairs may have created hazards.

Heating and Air-Conditioning Problems—Furnace defects (such as a cracked heat exchanger or malfunctioning controls), leaky boilers, uneven heat distribution, or inoperative emergency switches can spell trouble. A central air-conditioning unit that does not cool properly can be expensive to repair, especially if the compressor needs replacing.

Insulation and Ventilation Problems—Improper ventilation (such as sealed windows or unvented bathroom areas) can lead to both structural and cosmetic problems such as failure or rotting of components, or the growth of fungi or molds.

Maintenance Problems—A home that has been poorly maintained is generally a home to be avoided. If a home hasn't been taken care of on the surface, it could point to deeper neglect elsewhere. Renovations or repairs that were not professionally completed, such as structural, electrical, and plumbing, can lead to other problems.

Understanding the Report

No later than a few days after the inspection is complete, you should receive a report from the inspector. If you attended the inspection, the report will probably be easier to understand and you will probably get more out of it because you will have seen the items and their condition firsthand. The report might be as brief as a checklist of the condition of the items inspected, for example, "Hot Water Heater: ( ) Excellent ( ) Good ( ) Fair (X) Poor," or it might include additional details in a narrative report, as in "Hot water

smart step

Some contracts specify a time frame during which the buyer's inspection must occur, or the buyer forfeits the right to an inspection before closing. If your contract does, make sure you understand the time frame and act accordingly.

heater is nine years old and plastic particles were found in faucet aerators, indicating a potential dip tube problem. Due to age, recommend replacement of heater and flushing of water supply lines." It is far more helpful for you to receive a report that states what is wrong, why it is wrong, and what should be done about it. A form with a check stating that a water heater is in poor condition helps less than a report that explains why the water heater is in poor condition and whether or not it should be replaced. The report should inform you about the overall condition of the home and its many systems.

The report should reveal what repairs are needed and the urgency of those repairs. You should learn if there are any safety issues that need attention. If anything is wrong with an item or a system, you should learn from the report what needs to be done to correct the problem(s), what alternatives are available, the priority to assign each issue, whether there might be any concealed damage, whether further investigation is recommended, and the anticipated costs to repair.

After the Inspection

After you have reviewed the home inspection report, you should have a good idea of the overall condition of the home and its systems. Some of the systems reviewed may have a positive grade and some negative, but either way at least you will know where you stand. The report should describe the current condition of the home and should help you estimate any future expenses if you decide to proceed with the purchase. After reading the report, if you have any questions about it, call the inspector for additional information or clarification.

The home inspection reports what is currently found and does not guarantee the home against future problems. But remember this, too: No home is or ever

THE CHALLENGE

Maurice and Tanya find a home they like. The house is in a great neighborhood and is close to good schools, and the asking price seems reasonable. The couple makes an offer that is slightly below the owner's asking price of $133,000, and their offer contains a home inspection contingency. The home looks great, so the couple doesn't expect the inspection to turn up anything significant. When they receive the inspection report, they are surprised to learn that the roof is old and is leaking. The report recommends that it be replaced. Maurice and Tanya find out that replacing the roof costs about $6,000. Even so, Maurice and Tanya want the home, because other than the roof, it seems perfect for their needs.

THE PLAN

The couple's real estate agent suggests talking to the owner to determine if he will pay for the cost of the repairs or discount the price of the home. But the owner is unwilling to negotiate, and he indicates that he has already discounted the price of the home because of the age of the home. He also suggests that the contractor's estimate on the roof repair is too expensive. Maurice and Tanya call around some more and find that the original estimate for replacing the roof is accurate. The negotiation has reached an impasse, and neither side is willing to budge.

Maurice and Tanya want the home, but they feel that the owner is trying to take advantage of them. Although it is a difficult choice, they decide they will walk away from the deal if the issue can't be resolved. Their agent suggests the couple try one more time to negotiate with the owner. This time Maurice and Tanya offer to split the cost of the roof replacement with the owner. They also inform him that if a compromise can't be reached, they will walk away from the deal.

Although the owner still believes he is offering the home for a fair price, once he sees that they are serious about walking away, he agrees to split the cost of the roof replacement because he needs to sell the home. In the end, Maurice and Tanya get the home they want, with a new roof, and the owner gets almost all the money he expected from the sale of the home.

An estimated
92 percent of
U.S. homes
contain smoke
detectors, but
approximately
one-third of the
devices do not
work properly.

will be perfect. It is probable that the inspection will find something wrong with the home; homes are large, complicated systems and it is to be expected that there will be some problems. If the inspection does find some flaws with the home, it does not necessarily follow that you shouldn't buy the home. The report describes the degree of any problem discovered and the cost to correct the problem. A thorough home inspection will help you to analyze the situation and put you in a much better position to make informed decisions.

If your offer made the sale contingent upon the home passing the inspection (and it should have) and if the report uncovers something significant, you have three options.

First, you can call off the deal and walk away from the contract. That is why having a home inspection contingency protects you. Second, you can ask the seller to make or pay for the necessary repairs. If he or she doesn't, again, you can probably walk away. Finally, you can renegotiate the deal to take into account what it will cost you to repair the problems.

Don't expect your inspector to offer to fix what he finds. Inspectors are not repairmen. How much would you trust a report if you knew the inspector was trying to sell you on hiring him or her to repair whatever was uncovered? Because that would be a clear conflict of interest, home inspectors should not repair the problems they uncover. Seek out qualified contractors for any repair work needed and, as always, thoroughly check them out before hiring.

What if the report discovered nothing major? Congratulations! You can go forward with the sale and closing knowing the condition of the home you are buying. You will know your new home much better (especially if you accompanied the inspector), and the report should serve as a handy guide for future reference as you maintain your home.

the ESSENTIALS

1   A complete and thorough home inspection will assess the current condition of the home you are considering purchasing, before you actually purchase it.

2   A qualified home inspector will have a combination of training, knowledge, and experience that will enable him or her to accurately assess the condition of the home.

3   The inspection should cover all major components and systems of the home.

4   The report should assess and describe the condition of the home, document any safety issues, and reveal what needs to be done to correct any problems.

5   If the report turns up something significant, you can call off the deal, ask the seller to fix or pay for the problem to be fixed, or renegotiate the deal to account for what it will cost you to fix the problem.

smart step

Attend the inspection of your home so you can learn more about your home, get a firsthand look at any issues, and discuss the findings with your inspector.

9 [ATTENTION TO DETAIL:

Making Sure Nothing Goes Wrong]

"If anything can go wrong, it will."   —Murphy's Law

You have signed the contract and have had the home inspected. What next? There is still much to do to keep the deal moving forward. A sale of real estate is a complicated procedure, and there are still many tasks to complete. Your loan has to come through, contingencies have to be cleared up, maybe your present home has to sell, escrow needs to open, and so forth. There's a lot to do, and this chapter should help you move the process along.

Coping with Contingencies

Let's begin with the contingencies. If any contingencies are unresolved or otherwise not satisfactorily eliminated by the time of the closing, the sale won't close and the deal can't conclude. The two most common types of contingencies are those for financing and inspections.

The Financing Contingency—A financing contingency protects the buyer. If you are unable to get the necessary funding, the financing contingency allows you to get out of the contract. Can you imagine being obligated to buy a home but not being able to get a loan? Avoiding that disaster is the purpose of the financing contingency.

If you have already been preapproved for a loan, your loan approval should go smoothly. But many buyers, while preapproved, still need to get their loan approved. Once you have applied for the actual loan, the lender will ask you for various documents to back up your application, including recent bank statements, tax returns, proof of income, and so forth. Your job is to get them whatever they need when they want it. The lender wants to know that you qualify for the amount of the loan you are requesting.

Once you submit all requested material, your application, along with all related documents, is packaged and sent to a **loan underwriter**. The underwriter analyzes your information and determines if you, and the property to be purchased, meet the lender's financial criteria. What does the underwriter look at?

- **Your ability and willingness to pay the loan, including your overall creditworthiness**
- **Your ability to pay closing costs**
- **The condition and value of the property**

Upon conclusion of this analysis, the loan underwriter decides whether to approve, suspend, or deny your loan application. A suspension occurs when the underwriter feels that additional information is needed. For example, he or she might ask for:

- **A missing W-2 form**
- **Lawsuit documentation**
- **Prior bankruptcy documents**
- **Explanation of financial statements**

After the underwriter is finished, the loan package is forwarded to the closing department, where any last details are resolved and any last requirements handled prior to the date of your closing. Once all conditions have been resolved, all details ironed out, and any other outstanding issues resolved, you will be given a dollar amount for your closing costs. (See Chapter 10 for more details about closings.)

From beginning to end, the loan approval process should take between thirty and forty-five days. Can anything hold up this process? You bet! If you fail to answer the lender's questions sufficiently or in a timely manner, the process will bog down. If you fail to provide the requested documentation, the loan can collapse.

The Inspection Contingency—Like the financing contingency, the inspection contingency protects the buyer. Again, imagine the problems you would face if

smart step

When purchasing a home, feel free to seek advice and counsel from others, including real estate professionals, but make sure that the final decision is the right one for you.

smart step

Before purchasing a home, have a thorough inspection performed, by a qualified inspector, to ensure there are no hidden surprises.

you were forced to buy a home whose foundation, for example, was crumbling. Drastic problems are not unheard of, but far more common is finding out that several small things are wrong with the home. As discussed in Chapter 8, problems may give you the right to cancel the contract, but it is more common for buyers and sellers to find a mutually agreeable solution. Normally, the questions will be: Can the item be repaired or does it need to be replaced and who is going to pay for it? Often, both sides have to compromise if the deal is to be completed.

Consider how much effort it took to get to the point where you are negotiating the finer points of purchasing a home, *and* how much time and energy it will take to get to this point again with a different home. That is why most issues are somehow resolved. People have already made plans to move, and walking away from the deal at this late stage could be harmful to everyone. Far more common is working out a compromise with the seller to resolve the issue so the contingency can be eliminated and the sale allowed to continue.

A Word about Contingencies

There are many contingencies that may be part of your contract. As with the rest of your deal, you have options if any of these contingencies materialize: You can either call off the deal or work with the seller to find a mutually agreeable solution, which could include an extension of time to clear the contingency. Here are examples of some potential contingencies:

- **Home Purchase**—Used if the seller needs to find a new home before selling his or her current home.
- **Home Sale**—Used if the buyer needs to sell his or her current home before closing on the new home.
- **Termite Inspection**—Used to determine if termites are present in the home.
- **Completion of Repairs**—Used to make sure that all agreed-upon repairs are completed satisfactorily.
- **Ability to Obtain Insurance**—Used to make sure that the buyer can actually obtain homeowner's insurance on the home.

- **Fair and Marketable Title**—Used to make sure the buyer receives clear title to the home.
- **Disclosure**—Used to make sure the seller discloses material issues or material facts about the home such as environmental hazards caused by lead paint or asbestos.
- **Final Construction**—Used to allow buyer to approve final work in the construction of a new home.
- **Contract Review**—Used to allow either party the ability to have all contracts reviewed by a lawyer, for example.
- **Right to Review**—Used to allow the buyer to review covenants, restrictions, etc.

Generally speaking, you will want to work something out. The key is to know when a contingency is a deal-breaker. Typically, a sale is called off when a contingency will adversely and substantially affect the value of the home. Most contingencies are details that need to be handled and not emergencies requiring you to abandon ship. As such, most should be dealt with reasonably.

plain talk

Collateral is the property that secures a loan. A home is the collateral for a mortgage, as the vehicle is collateral for an auto loan.

Beyond contingencies, another item that can derail the deal is the possibility that the appraisal comes in too low.

The Appraisal—Before your loan is approved, the lending institution will want to see the property appraised at the sale price (or higher). If the home is appraised for less than the sale price, the lender can conclude that you are paying too much for the home and that its loan may not be properly secured. Remember, if you default, the home is the **collateral** for your loan. Lenders do not want to make a loan that is larger than the value of the collateral.

Generally, the lender will order the appraisal. Once the appraisal has been completed, you will want to make sure you receive a copy of it. The appraisal will contain a lot of information about the property you are purchasing and will also include items such as comparable properties and information about current

Fees for an
appraisal vary,
but generally
range from
$250 to $500
for a residential
property report.

market trends in the area. Remember, the purpose of the appraisal is to establish an accurate and impartial value for the property. Doing so can help assure that you aren't overpaying for the property in the current market and that the lender's interests are protected.

If you need to find an appraiser on your own, you can usually find one by asking your lender, agent, or lawyer. Look for an appraiser who is licensed by his or her state, experienced, and competent in conducting appraisals. Ask the appraiser about his or her knowledge of the area and experience appraising the type of property you are buying. As with the home inspector, you need to check up on the appraiser and be assured that he or she has the experience and qualifications to do a thorough, professional job.

The Appraisal Process

An appraisal is an independent analysis and opinion of the value of a home. It is not the replacement cost (for insurance purposes) and it is probably not the assessed value (for taxation purposes), although it may be close. An appraisal reflects the market value (what a willing buyer would pay a willing seller). Appraisers look at a variety of factors when they determine the value of a home.

✓ ————————————————————➤ **Appraisal Checklist**

- **Comparable home sales**
- **Age of the home**
- **Style of the home, design, layout, square footage**
- **Quality of construction**
- **Improvements made to the home**
- **Condition of the premises**
- **Easements, covenants, and assessments**

- [ ] **Condition and age of the neighborhood**
- [ ] **Zoning**
- [ ] **Supply and demand**
- [ ] **Access to schools, shopping, highways, and commercial areas**

By analyzing market data, comparable sales, current offers, pending sales, proposed improvements, and so on, the appraiser is able to compare your desired property to the overall market. To assess this, he or she may use county records, the Multiple Listing Service, market trends, discussions with local real estate professionals, and his or her own knowledge. Appraisers weigh different factors differently, but essentially, they compare your home to similar homes to come up with the property's **fair market value**

You can control much of the home buying process—you choose the home, the agent, the offer, the lender, the home inspector, and maybe even the appraiser—but you have almost no power over the actual appraisal. It is an independent third-party analysis of the home. The appraiser will know what you have agreed to pay, but that price should not affect his or her judgment. Normally, the appraisal is right on the mark; a low appraisal is the exception not the rule. Once the appraisal comes in, supporting the purchase price, the lender can issue its commitment letter and the closing can begin.

Dealing with a Low Appraisal

One of the worst things that can happen during the home buying process is the appraisal coming in too low. If this happens, the lender may refuse to fund the loan. As with almost everything else in the process, a low appraisal can be fixed and the deal salvaged. But what if that does happen? What if your appraisal comes in, say, $15,000 below the sales price? What do you do? Here are your options:

plain talk

The fair market value of a home, also known as the fair cash value or reasonable value, is the price of a home determined by parties that are ready and willing to do business.

Back Out of the Contract—Because of the financing contingency, a low appraisal likely means that you can get out of the contract. That is probably not your first choice, but it is good to know it is an option.

Ask the Seller to Reduce the Home's Price—A low appraisal can be used to the buyer's advantage. Because the owner also knows you can legally get out of the contract, and because the time for closing the sale is probably no more than a few weeks away, a low appraisal means that the owner may be willing to deal. Your seller may (however reluctantly) be willing to renegotiate. Would he or she be willing to reduce the sales price by $15,000? Maybe, so it never hurts to ask.

Pay More—If you really love the home, and if the appraisal is accurate, you may be willing to pay the difference. That is, you might be able to pay an extra $15,000 down, so the loan will again meet the appraised value.

Compromise—It may be that the seller has to take a little less and you have to make a larger down payment. If you can work something out, where each party bends a little, the deal may not end up being broken.

Dispute the Appraisal—Lenders are in the business of making loans. They want your loan to go through almost as much as you do. They have already expended considerable effort to approve your loan by this point. Therefore, they may be open to getting a second appraisal, and maybe even paying for it.

There are many reasons an appraisal may come in low. Some of those reasons may be valid, including that you offered too much for the home. But some of those reasons may be that the appraiser didn't accurately appraise the home. He or she may have used homes for comparison that were really not comparable, or may not have taken into account important aspects of the home. Adjustments can be made, if justified.

Once an accurate appraisal value has been established and the lender has agreed to fully fund the loan, it is time to close the sale.

Escrow and Title Companies

Often lumped together, escrow and title are distinctly separate things. What is the difference? An escrow officer is a neutral third party who coordinates the transfer of the property. It is sort of like two people who want to buy and sell a car. One says, "Give me the keys and I'll give you the money," while the other says, "Give me the money and I'll give you the keys." The solution is escrow. An escrow officer takes the keys from the seller and gives them to the buyer while simultaneously taking the money from the buyer and giving it to the seller. The escrow company collects the loan money from the lender and transfers it to the seller, and collects clear title from the title company and transfers the home to you. A title company is different. A title officer makes sure that the owner really owns the home and has clear title (free of any third-party liens, encumbrances, or judgments) to be able to sell it to you or another buyer.

Escrow and title are sometimes handled by the same company, but that is not always so. You (or your real estate agent) will need to open escrow and find a title company (unless the seller requires a specific escrow and title company), so you need to understand what each does and how it affects the outcome.

Escrow

The buyer, the seller, or an agent of either party can open escrow. By placing your good faith deposit into an escrow account, escrow is opened. The escrow holder may be an independent escrow company, a title company, an attorney, or some other closing agent authorized by your state.

THE CHALLENGE

Sara is hunting for a new home. She can afford a $175,000 mortgage and has $10,000 to put down on a home. She knows the neighborhood where she wants to live and knows that a three-bedroom home in that area of town should cost about $200,000. She feels that she is ready to find a new home. Sara scours the real estate ads and comes upon a listing that intrigues her: "3 BR, beautiful, needs a little work, $185,000." Sara is pretty handy and figures she can fix whatever problems there might be. It seems like she might be able to get a good deal on a home in the exact neighborhood she wants.

Sara goes to look at the home and is pleasantly surprised. The house needs some cosmetic repairs, which she feels she can handle, and some sprucing up. She decides to offer $175,000, figuring the deal will end up somewhere between the owner's original price and her offer. However, the owner is firm that he wants $185,000. Even at that price, Sara feels she is getting a good deal, so she enters into a contract for the home.

Sara opens escrow and is preliminarily approved for the loan. An appraisal is ordered. Sara is shocked when her loan officer contacts her to let her know that the appraised value came in at $165,000— $20,000 lower than the purchase price.

THE PLAN

Sara requests a copy of the appraisal and looks it over to see what had caused the big difference in value. After reading the report for a third time, Sara realizes that the appraiser hadn't accounted for the bedroom that had been added on to the home some five years earlier. She speaks with the appraiser, and he informs her that the owner had never gotten a permit from the city for the addition, so the appraiser can't take it into account. (An illegal addition may not be included in an appraisal. Legally speaking, it was as if the bedroom was never added on.) The appraiser seems to be right.

At Sara's request, the lender hires another appraiser. Although he agrees that the building is technically a two-bedroom home and not a three-bedroom property, the second appraiser nevertheless appraises the property at $175,000, largely because of the great neighborhood. Sara is still $10,000 off from the amount of the purchase price. Sara feels she had no other alternative and informs the seller that because of the low appraisal she would have to back out of the deal.

Sara was disappointed that she had finally found the home of her dreams and it now seemed to be slipping away. Alarmed that his home would not sell and fearing that the same issue might crop up again with the next potential buyer, the owner reluctantly agrees to reduce the purchase price to $175,000. Sara got her loan, and the deal for her new home went through.

The escrow company will assign an escrow officer to coordinate your purchase. This person will be your contact throughout the closing process. If you have questions or concerns about title, contingencies, or other such issues, your escrow officer (and real estate agent) should be able to resolve those issues.

Within the real estate contract that you and the seller signed is a provision for the scheduled escrow closing date. Normally, it is a date selected by agreement between the buyer and seller. The closing date should give both sides enough time to do everything they need to do (inspect the home, get an appraisal, find a new home, finalize the loan) before wrapping up the deal.

Your escrow officer will need to know the date the home is to close because he or she will be prorating various expenses and credits, such as interest, taxes, and insurance, up until the closing day.

If your loan processing takes longer than you expected, or your present home doesn't sell quickly enough (home sale contingency), or the seller can't get into another home on time (home purchase contingency), or there is some other reason why escrow needs to stay open longer than anticipated, the closing date can be extended. If either party needs to extend the closing date of the escrow, both parties must sign and agree to an extension of the original purchase agreement. (The actual closing of escrow is a complicated process and is discussed in detail in the next chapter.)

fast fact

Although escrow officers are not lawyers, they are trained in real-estate procedures, title insurance, taxes, deeds, and relevant regulations.

Title

What if, after selling his home to you, your seller turned around and sold it to someone else a week later? And what if that person paid cash and closed escrow in a week? Such transactions are rare, but not unheard of. Or consider this scenario: You agree to buy a home without knowing that it is in the process of being seized by the IRS.

This is why you need a title company to perform a title search, and why your lender requires a title search. A title company reviews the records of the county assessor, the county recorder, and other government agencies as they relate to the parcel to locate any documents that might negatively affect clear and marketable title. A title search will take anywhere from an hour to a few weeks to complete. For the transaction to conclude, the seller must provide the buyer a clear title with no "clouds" on it. A title might be clouded (and, therefore, not clear) if, for instance, there is a tax **lien** against the property.

There are several types of liens, each of which can cloud the title:

- **Judgment lien.** When a defendant in a lawsuit is sued and loses, the court issues a judgment against that defendant. When that judgment is later recorded against the defendant's real estate, it is called a judgment lien. It must be paid before the property can be transferred.
- **Mechanics or construction lien.** This is a claim made by a contractor or subcontractor who has performed work on the home and who has yet to be paid.
- **Divorce-related lien.** When one spouse is awarded a home in a divorce and is required to pay the other spouse a share of the proceeds upon the sale of the home, the other spouse can file a lien for his or her share against the home.
- **Child-support lien.** In some states, if a spouse is owed unpaid child support, he or she can place a lien on the ex-spouse's realty.
- **Homeowners' Association lien.** If you are buying a home that is part of a homeowners' association, there may be a lien against it for past-due association dues or other assessments.

If there is a lien on the property you are buying, the owner must pay off the debt to remove the cloud from the title. The owner must also get a lien release and have it recorded in the county recorder's office at or before closing.

Title Insurance

Even if there are no liens against the property you want to buy, you may be required to obtain title insurance. Title insurance protects you and the lender against clouds on the title that may have occurred long ago and which were not visible during the routine title search. For example, your title to the property may have been forged years ago (meaning, you are not really the owner now), or there may have been clerical errors, undisclosed heirs with an earlier claim to the property, incorrect marking of the boundaries, an earlier transfer signature by a minor, incorrect interpretation of a will, or any number of potential claims against the property by some unknown third party. Title insurance protects you against these potential losses.

The odds are that you will never have to file a claim against your title insurance carrier, but if you do, you will be happy you have this valuable insurance. The cost is minimal compared to the protection it provides.

Things can and do go wrong during the purchase of a home, but there are steps you can take to minimize your risk. Contingencies, such as for financing and inspection, protect your interests should anything go wrong. If contingency-related problems do arise, you can either get the problems fixed or back out of the deal. Once all contingencies have been resolved, it is time to close your deal.

Contracts for the sale of real estate must be in writing, and any amendments to that contract must be in writing as well to be legal.

the ESSENTIALS

1 A financing contingency protects you if you are unable to get a loan to purchase the home. Keep in mind that providing the lender everything it needs to back up your application dramatically increases your chances of getting the loan.

2 An inspection contingency protects you if problems are discovered during the inspection. The deal can be cancelled if necessary, but

generally, the buyer and seller renegotiate the deal to account for repairing or replacing whatever caused the problem.

3 An appraisal is performed to establish an accurate and impartial value for the property. Appraising the property can help ensure that you aren't overpaying for it and that the lender's interests are protected.

4 Opening escrow occurs when your good faith deposit is given to a neutral third party to be held for safekeeping during the home buying process.

5 Title insurance protects against disputes over ownership of the property, such as if the previous owner did not have clear title to the property when it was sold.

10 [DOTTING I'S, CROSSING T'S:

All about the Closing]

"It ain't over 'til it's over."

—Yogi Berra

When the pre-
vious owner
wants to stay
in the home for
an extra month
or two after
closing and
pays rent to
the new owner,
it is called a
rent-back.

The final step after the contract has been signed and the home has been inspected is the closing. At closing, ownership of the home is transferred to the buyer and the money is transferred to the seller. Depending upon which state you live in, this may occur at the office of an escrow company, a title office, or the office of a real estate agent or a lawyer. (For our purposes, we will call the person conducting the closing the "escrow officer.") But before you get to the closing, many details still need attention and yet more hoops need to be jumped through. In this chapter we will give you some insight on how to clear those final hurdles and get to the finish line with a minimum of fuss.

Scheduling the Closing

A home closing usually occurs between thirty and sixty days after the signing of the purchase agreement. It can happen sooner: If you are an all-cash buyer and there are no contingencies, closing can occur in a week. It can also take longer: In rare instances, a ninety-day closing date may be agreed upon if, for example, you need extra time to sell your present home. The problem with a lengthened closing schedule is that it allows more time for things to go wrong. In most cases, completing the sale sooner is better.

Sometimes buyers and sellers have a hard time agreeing on a closing date. For example, it may be that the sellers can't move into their new home for sixty days, but you would like to occupy your new home in thirty days. Normally, these sorts of scheduling conflicts can be agreeably resolved. For example, the new owners might allow the old owners to **rent back** the home for a month. Scheduling problems can also act in your favor, financially speaking. If you have any leeway in your move-in date, you can offer to accommodate the seller and close in thirty days, but then rent the home back to the now ex-owners for another thirty days beyond that. The amount of rent is negotiable and should provide you with some compensation for being flexible with your move-in date.

Preparing for the Closing

After all contingencies have been handled, the loan has received final approval, and the closing date is set, there are still a few things left to do before the actual closing:

Homeowner's Insurance—You will not be able to close your deal unless you have insurance for the home. Call your insurance professional to review your coverage needs, explore your options and the associated costs, and then purchase a policy. You will need to bring proof of insurance to the closing. This generally takes the form of an **evidence of insurance** document and provides evidence that the insurance company is insuring your home. The lender will want to make sure that it is listed as a mortgagee (the party loaning money toward the purchase of the home) on the policy in case something should happen to the home.

Contingency Follow-Up—All contingencies, such as the seller making any agreed-upon repairs, must be satisfactorily resolved before closing.

Arrange for the Final Walk-Through—Before the closing, it is smart and customary for the buyer to make a final walk-through of the property. This gives you a chance to obtain the instruction manuals for items such as the appliances, security system, or irrigation system. More importantly, a walk-through is a chance to check that the home is in the condition you anticipate it should be in. Is it in the same condition as when you last saw it? Were the repairs completed? What if the answer is "no"? What if that old boat is still in the backyard? When things are amiss, it is generally because the seller was negligent or because there may have been some miscommunication. Whatever the reason, you have two choices.

First, you can delay the closing until everything is as it should be. Unfortunately, this tactic might anger the seller, especially if the problem is due to a miscom-

plain talk

Evidence of insurance proves you have an insurance policy in place on the home you are purchasing.

munication. When the deal is closing and people get angry, the deal may collapse. That is why the second option may be better: Find a way to work it out.

Maybe the buyer will agree to pay a little less and do the work himself. Maybe the seller will agree to have the sale proceeds left in escrow until the repairs are completed. Compromise is necessary and everything is negotiable. Making an enemy of the seller is usually not a good idea. But you won't know where things stand unless you have a final walk-through.

Obtain the Settlement Statement—The settlement statement details how much cash you will need to bring to the closing (for fees and costs), specifies loan details, explains how funds will be dispersed, and allows you to review the financial aspects of the closing. Ask your escrow officer for the settlement statement a week before the scheduled closing. You probably won't get the document that early, but it is best to put the wheels in motion. Even if you receive the statement two days before the closing, it will still help you prepare. Legally, you have a right to review (upon request) the settlement statement one business day before the closing.

Get Certified Funds—The settlement statement specifies how much money you must have ready to close the deal. The escrow officer will not accept a personal check; you must have certified funds ready.

Contact the Movers—At least a month before you want to move, you should contact some movers, get estimates, check references, and schedule the move.

Call Utility Companies—Have the utilities transferred into your name at the new address as of the settlement date or, if you rent the home back to the seller, your occupancy date.

Go to the Post Office—Submit a change of address form to the post office and notify anyone who may need your new address.

How the Closing Works

Once the closing place and time have been settled, the escrow officer will coordinate the activities of the buyer, seller, lender, and other parties involved. He or she will collect all closing documents and distribute them to the real estate agents, lawyers, and/or principals involved.

Different states have different requirements, but here is a list of the documents you will most likely encounter at your closing:

The Deed—The deed is the legal document that transfers ownership from the seller to the buyer. The seller brings the deed to the closing, where it will be signed and notarized. The escrow officer will record the deed with the county after the closing has been completed, making the transfer a public record.

The Settlement Statement—The settlement statement (required by federal law) itemizes the loan and lists the charges to the buyer and the seller. It has to be signed by both the buyer and the seller at the closing.

The Loan Documents—The loan documents list the terms of the loan, including the monthly payment amount, due dates, penalties for late payments, and where payments should be sent.

The Mortgage or Deed of Trust—Depending upon what state you are in, you will have either a mortgage or a deed of trust securing the loan. This gives the lender a claim against your home and the right to foreclose on it should you default on the note. The mortgage or deed of trust will reference the note specifics again and will obligate you to pay your principal, interest, taxes, and insurance on time, to maintain homeowner's insurance on the property, and to not allow the property to deteriorate. If you default on these obligations, the mortgage allows the lender to demand full payment of your loan balance im-

fast fact

The federal Real Estate Settlement Procedures Act (RESPA) requires the HUD-1 Settlement Statement be used "as the standard real estate settlement form in all transactions in the United States which involve federally related mortgage loans."

mediately, to foreclose, to sell the property, and to use the proceeds to pay off the loan and costs of foreclosure.

The Truth-in-Lending (TIL) Statement—The TIL provides you with information about your loan including the Annual Percentage Rate (APR), the interest rate on an annual basis, associated with how much your credit is going to cost you when all charges and fees are included. This document should be familiar to you as federal law mandates that your lender provide it within three days of your loan application. The final TIL statement may not (and probably won't) match the initial TIL statement you received after applying for your loan. If any items have changed, make sure you agree with them before signing anything.

Affidavits—Affidavits, or declarations, are sworn oaths, made under penalty of perjury. Affidavits may be required by the lender and by your state. There are different affidavits for different purposes. You might have to sign one, for example, stating that you will be occupying the home.

Closing

The big day has finally arrived. You are due to close on your home. Congratulations! On this day, you will deposit any remaining money due into escrow and sign the escrow and loan documents. Your seller will sign the deed over to you and receive a check for the money due to him or her. The deed will be recorded that day. One more thing will also happen on this day: At the end of the day, you will own a home.

In some states, the seller and buyer proceed through the closing process separately, while in others, you sit in a room together. The actual process can take anywhere from an hour to several hours, depending on the situation. The

WHO PAYS WHAT?			
	BUYER	SELLER	EXPLANATION
Closing Fee	✓	✓	For the preparation and handling of the closing documents.
Recording Fee	✓	✓	For the recording of the mortgage and deed.
Real Estate Commissions		✓	Seller pays for both agents, normally 6 percent of the sales price.
Title Search Fee		✓	The search allows the seller to show the required marketable title.
Title Insurance	✓	✓	Depending upon where you live.
Mortgage Payoff		✓	Seller's present loan is paid off by the sale proceeds.
Tax Prorating	✓		Reimbursement to the seller for pending property taxes.
Prepaid Interest and Escrow Deposits	✓		Prepaid interest on the loan and any deposits needed for insurance and taxes.
Loan Closing Costs	✓		For the appraisal, credit report, document preparation, underwriting, and closing fees.
Inspection Costs	✓		For the termite inspection, property survey, etc.

smart step

Don't make the mistake of thinking the cheapest mover is always the way to go. Broken, stolen, or lost items and late deliveries can make you wish you hadn't shopped on price alone.

escrow officer will go over the mortgage with the buyer, notarize the signatures, have the seller sign the deed, and so on. The time-consuming part is going over all the loan documents and required disclosures. The documents can be intimidating. Be sure to have all your questions answered because the documents you are signing obligate you to pay a lot of money for a long time.

The most confusing part of this process may be understanding the costs associated with closing a home purchase and determining who pays what.

Keeping Closing Costs Down

Unanticipated closing costs are common, but they are always a big shock to homebuyers. Imagine thinking that you need $7,000 to close your home, only to learn that you are going to be $2,500 short because you hadn't accounted for needing flood insurance, loan points, a home warranty premium, or the many document preparation fees.

Here are some ways to reduce your closing costs:

Apply for a No-Point Loan—If you elect to take a no-point loan you may have to pay a higher interest rate, but paying no points means that you won't pay any points at closing. On a $150,000 loan, two points equals $3,000 that you can shave off your closing costs.

Schedule Your Closing for Late in the Month—At closing, lenders are paid interest for the remainder of the month. If you close on the 10th, you will owe interest on your loan for another twenty days. But if you close on the 28th, you will owe interest only for those two days that remain in the month. Closing at the end of the month can reduce your closing costs quite a bit.

Get a "Rebate" from the Seller for Your Closing Costs—For example, if you agree to pay $150,000 for the home, you can raise your offer by the amount you will need to close, and then get the seller to credit that amount back to you at the closing. Many lenders restrict this practice to between 3 and 6 percent of the purchase price and the appraisal must support the increase in price.

In our example, if you agree to buy the home for $150,000, you could ask the seller if he or she would increase the sale price by 5 percent, or $7,500, to $157,500. You would get a loan for that amount, and at closing, the seller would credit you the extra $7,500 for closing costs. The seller still gets

$150,000 and, in essence, you prorate your $7,500 closing costs over the length of your loan.

The Impound Account

Another unexpected expense you may encounter is the impound account. Also called a reserve or escrow account, an impound account is an account set up by your lender to collect money from you to pay future property tax and insurance bills.

Here's how it works: After you close, you may be required to pay future property taxes and insurance premiums into the account, usually every month as part of your monthly payment. When the bills come due, the lender will pay the property tax and insurance charges on your home out of this account.

The good news about impound accounts is that they force you to pay your taxes and insurance, which is good for people on tight budgets. Even if your lender does not require an impound account, you might want to set one up anyway. They force you to pay bills on time. But if you prefer to pay these costs directly to the taxing authority and the insurance company, and have the full use of your money until the bills are due, you may be able to avoid having an impound account altogether. But do put the money away to pay the bills when they come due. If you don't, you could find it difficult to pay for them.

Transferring Title

Title is equivalent to ownership. When the title to a home is in your name, you own the home. What most homebuyers don't know is that title can be held in different legal ways, and how you hold title determines what you can do with the property and who inherits it if you pass away.

THE CHALLENGE

Marty and Sandy are ready to buy their first home. They have $10,000 for a down payment and have another $3,000 for closing costs. After evaluating their mortgage options, they settle on a mortgage that does not require paying any points. They realize that that they will pay a higher interest rate, but they simply can't afford to put more money down and need to keep their closing costs as low as possible.

Marty asks the escrow officer for the settlement statement several times in the week leading up to the closing. Each time he is told the statement isn't ready. Finally, the day before the closing, the escrow officer calls Marty to tell him that the statement is ready. After picking it up, Marty and Sandy are shocked to discover that the closing is going to cost another $1,200; the escrow company had added some additional fees and they were being charged for the home warranty.

THE PLAN

Marty's first plan is to be nice. He explains to the escrow officer that they simply have no more money to put down on the home. He asks if the escrow officer can waive the extra charges. The escrow officer replies that it isn't possible to waive the fee and that Marty must find the money somewhere. Marty then takes a stand. He retorts that he and Sandy will refuse to sign if the charges aren't waived. He isn't kidding and storms out of the office. The deal is on the verge of collapse.

Marty also calls their real estate agent to discuss the situation. In addition to the fees that had been added, there has been a misunderstanding about whether or not the seller is going to pay for the home warranty as part of the deal.

The real estate agent knows that everyone has put too much time and energy into the deal to see it fall apart at this late date. She calls the escrow officer and tries to work something out. After a bit of negotiation, Marty's real estate agent agrees to take $600 less in commission, the escrow officer waives another $600 in charges, and the deal closes as scheduled the next day.

You may be thinking, this doesn't apply to me. I have a will. I am giving the home to my sister. Wrong. Title to a home trumps any will, and if you hold title in a way that doesn't allow you to transfer it to your sister, your sister is going to be out of luck. So title is an important concept to understand. You need to tell the title officer or escrow officer how you want title held in the new deed.

There are four ways to legally hold title to real estate. The first is used when you buy property alone. The other three are your options when you buy it with someone else (a spouse or business partner, for example).

1. **Sole and Separate Property**—When you buy property alone, the title will be put in your name alone as the sole and separate owner. This means that the property is yours to do with as you like.
2. **Joint Tenancy**—The distinguishing characteristic of this form of title (also sometimes called "joint tenancy with a right of survivorship") is that you are joint owners with another party, and when you die, the other party will own the property totally. If you buy property with a business partner, and you want to will your half to your wife upon your death, you can't if title is held this way. When one joint tenant dies, his or her share *automatically* goes to the other joint tenant.
3. **Tenants in Common**—Tenants in common divide ownership of property equally. If one owner dies, his or her share does not automatically go to the other tenant in common, as it does with a joint tenancy. Rather, the deceased tenant's 50 percent share will go to whomever that tenant designated prior to death. Each tenant has equal right to possess the property as well.
4. **Community Property**—This type of ownership is available only to married couples in the nine community property states: Arizona, California, Idaho, Louisiana, Nevada, New Mexico, Texas, Washington, and Wisconsin. In this arrangement, both spouses have an equal right to possess the property during their marriage.

Upon the death of either spouse, the other spouse receives the deceased's share. It is not unlike joint tenancy in that regard.

How you hold title has legal, tax, and estate planning ramifications. Speak with your lawyer and tax professional to make sure you are making the right decision.

Moving In

Most buyers take possession of their new homes immediately after closing, unless they are renting the homes back to the sellers. The keys and garage door opener are handed over at the closing because the home has officially changed owners. In some states, the seller may retain possession for up to five days after closing, but even there, the custom is to be out of the house by closing. Now, after you have done the research, found the right home, had it inspected and appraised, obtained financing, and made it through closing, it's time to say, Welcome to your new home!

the ESSENTIALS

1   There are many details to handle before the closing, such as getting homeowner's insurance. Start early, so you will be prepared.

2   At the closing, you will be given many documents to review and sign. Understanding what each is beforehand can make the process less intimidating.

3   There are many fees associated with the closing, some of which can be reduced if you know what to expect beforehand. Knowing who pays what will help you avoid paying unexpected fees.

4 How you hold title to your new home is important. Talk to your lawyer to determine what is right for you.

5 Buying a home is a huge financial commitment, so it is a good idea to review all closing documents with your lawyer.

smart step

Start Now!

Calculate what it is worth to reduce your spending in order to save more for your home purchase.

Log on to
hrblock.com/advisor

11 [BE PREPARED!:

Insuring Your Investment]

"Things turn out best for people who make the best out of the way things turn out."
—John Wooden

Life holds a lot of uncertainty. Just about everything is uncertain except perhaps death and taxes. For example, you don't know if a tornado will strike your home, if a thief will break in to rob you, or if your dog will decide to bite someone. Each of these events is different, but they all have one thing in common: financial consequences. You can decide to accept the financial consequences associated with future risks or you can minimize your potential losses by sharing the risks with an insurance company. Managing risk is what insurance is all about.

Part of managing risk is being prepared. For your home, you'll want that preparation to include homeowner's insurance in case a calamity strikes your home. There is nothing magical about homeowner's insurance. It can't protect your home from being destroyed in a tornado and it can't stop a thief from breaking in to rob you, but it can help prevent whatever calamity strikes your home from destroying you financially.

Homeowner's insurance is something you need, even if you never need to use it. It is your protection if something bad happens: a fire, a theft, an accident on your property—that sort of thing. It seems simple enough, but unfortunately it is not. There are a number of different policies and related **exclusions** that define what is, and is not, covered. In this chapter, we will cover some of the basics.

Homeowner's Insurance 101

Homeowner's insurance can be broken down into two basic parts: property and liability. Property coverage insures you for loss or damage to the structure and its contents caused by perils (the specific cause of loss or damage) such as fire, hail, or theft. Liability coverage protects you in case you become liable for someone else's injuries, if, for example, your neighbor slips and falls on your steps or your dog bites someone.

Lenders require homebuyers to buy coverage to protect their interests. If the home is damaged or destroyed by fire, storms, vandals, or other disasters covered in the policy, the insurance company will provide the money to repair or replace the home. The minimum level of coverage required by the lender will protect the value of repairing or replacing the structure, but it might not cover all your personal belongings inside. To protect *all* your financial interests, you need to obtain adequate coverage based on your personal needs.

Areas of Coverage

There are several types of homeowner's insurance policies. The policies are similar (policies' coverage may vary by state), and the differences are limited to how much they cost and what they cover. Policies with greater or broader coverage generally cost more, but they also provide more protection.

A typical or standard homeowner's insurance policy offers coverage in several different areas. Generally, you also have the option to add additional coverage or extend or increase the coverage that is included.

Property—This covers your home and separate structures that are not attached to your home, such as a gazebo or detached garage or shed. The amount of coverage for these separate structures can vary, but it is generally about 10 percent of the amount of coverage on the home itself.

Personal Property—Personal property, such as household furnishings, clothing, and other personal belongings, is covered by this type of insurance. The amount of coverage you have for these items is based on the amount of coverage you have on the home itself, and generally the minimum coverage is 50 percent. Most policies include coverage of your personal property should a covered loss such as theft occur anywhere in the world.

fast fact

The effective date of your policy determines when your insurance policy (coverage) goes into effect, and the expiration date determines when your policy (coverage) ends.

Personal Liability—This covers bodily injuries to other people or damage to their property should you become liable. It covers both the cost of the injury or damage as well as the cost of related lawsuits. Because the cost of claims continues to rise, you may need to increase the amount of coverage beyond what is included as a standard amount in the policy.

Additional Living Expenses—This coverage pays for the additional costs associated with living away from your home because of damage from a covered loss. The amount of coverage can vary and generally includes items such as meals, lodging, and other related expenses.

Extra or Supplemental Coverage—This coverage *is not* part of your basic homeowner's policy, but you may want to consider purchasing it to be adequately insured. Extra coverage increases the amount of coverage in your policy, and supplemental coverage gives you coverage that is not ordinarily included in your policy. Examples of extra coverage might include a personal articles **floater**, which extends the coverage on certain valuables such as jewelry or collections, or an umbrella policy, which increases the amount of coverage for personal liability. Supplemental coverage might include flood or earthquake insurance, which is not normally covered in typical policies.

Types of Homeowner's Insurance Policies

There are many types of homeowner's insurance policies from which to choose. You will hear the policies referred to by their form number, such as HO-3 (Homeowner's 3). Also known as the special form, this is the most popular policy because it covers all perils (all risks) unless they are specifically excluded from coverage. Coverage for your personal property can also vary by form and be covered on a named-peril or all-peril basis. Consult with your insurance professional to determine which form and type of coverage is right for you. Here is an overview of some of the forms available:

- **HO-1.** This is a basic (limited) homeowner's policy that provides coverage against eleven specifically named perils. This policy is being phased out and is no longer available in many states.
- **HO-2.** Commonly known as a broad form policy, this homeowner's policy provides coverage for seventeen specifically named perils.
- **HO-3.** Referred to as a special form policy, this policy is an all-peril (all-risk) policy that provides coverage for all risks unless specifically excluded. The majority of homeowners select this form for the extensive coverage it provides.
- **HO-4.** This policy is commonly known as renter's insurance and does not provide coverage for the structure of the building. It provides personal property and personal liability coverage.
- **HO-5.** This policy provides extensive homeowner's coverage with few exclusions. The main difference is how your personal property is covered. It is covered for replacement cost if the loss is caused by a covered peril.
- **HO-6.** This policy is similar to renter's insurance. It is intended for people living in a co-op or condominium.
- **HO-8.** This is a policy that is designed for older homes or those that don't meet certain underwriting standards associated with the other forms.

fast fact

A named-peril policy provides coverage for only those perils listed, while an all-peril (all-risk) policy provides coverage for all perils except for those specifically excluded.

—— When It Rains, It Pours, So Do You Need an Umbrella?

So you've covered all of your bases by purchasing insurance coverage for claims you may become liable for, but will it be enough coverage? With today's sky-rocketing liability costs, how can you be sure? Say, for example, a guest in your home accidentally gets hurt and you are liable for damages that are in excess of the limits of your policy. Do you have other assets (such as your savings account) you would like to use to pay for the damages? If not, you may want to help protect the rest of your assets against a large claim that exceeds the limits of your

The limits of
the policy are
the maximum
amounts the
insurance com-
pany will pay in
the event of a
covered loss.

policy by purchasing umbrella coverage. Umbrella coverage provides just what the name implies: coverage over your other policies. It kicks in after the basic liability of the other policies it covers has been exhausted and usually has a limit of $1 million or more. This coverage is added on top of the limit for other policies it covers (such as homeowner's or automobile). Best of all, this large amount of coverage can be relatively inexpensive to acquire. See your insurance professional for more information.

Replacement Cost or Actual Cash Value?

After you have decided which policy to purchase, if something happens, you don't have to worry, right? Well, if something actually happens (and unfortunately things do happen) to your home or personal property, would you be able to repair the damage or replace the item if it were totally destroyed? It depends upon how you chose reimbursement in the case of damage or loss.

Reimbursements are available in two ways: You can insure your home and its contents for replacement cost or actual cash value (ACV). Replacement cost coverage pays to have the damage repaired or replaced with similar materials, whereas actual cash value is the replacement cost less depreciation, or the decrease in value due to age, wear and tear, etc. If you choose ACV, you may not receive enough money to repair the damage or replace the home or item as costs continue to rise. Even with replacement cost coverage, certain factors, such as rising material and construction costs or rebuilding the home to meet new building codes, could push the costs associated with the damage above the **limits** of your policy.

Some companies offer extended or guaranteed replacement cost coverage that increases the amount of coverage above the limits stated in the policy. Replacement cost is somewhat more expensive, but carefully consider what would happen if you actually suffered a loss. Bottom line, you'll want to make sure you are adequately covered if your home and its contents are damaged or destroyed.

How Much Coverage Is Enough?

Once you understand the types and levels of coverage that are available, you can make an informed decision about what is right for you. Your goal should be to buy enough insurance so you are adequately protected in the event of a loss. When looking at insurance coverage, focus on removing or reducing the financial risks associated with the big calamities. Your insurance coverage should take care of the big financial losses you can't handle on your own.

When you are evaluating your options and the level of coverage you'll need, consider the following:

- **Your home.** Consider the amount of your mortgage, the cost to repair or replace the structure, and any separate structures, such as an unattached garage.
- **Your personal property.** Consider the furnishings in your home, your clothes, and any other personal belongings you have.
- **Your personal liability.** Consider how expensive lawsuits and damage awards have become if you become liable for someone else's injuries or damage to their property.
- **Your living expenses.** Consider how much it would cost to buy food and shelter if you couldn't live in your home because it had been damaged or destroyed.

Prior to closing, your lender will require proof of insurance coverage from your insurance company indicating you have coverage on the home. The statement is called evidence of insurance.

Understanding your coverage options and determining an appropriate and adequate level of coverage can seem overwhelming. But this is an important step in protecting one of your greatest and most important investments. Your insurance professional can provide a great deal of assistance in making sure you're adequately protected and can also give you information and tips to help prevent or minimize the losses that do occur.

Calculating Your Insurance Costs

There are a variety of factors that will affect the amount of your homeowner's insurance **premium**. Some are fairly obvious, while others are not, but all work together to determine how much each type of coverage costs. Let's take a look at some of them now.

The Home—Factors that affect premiums include the size of your home (square footage), the style of your home (ranch, two story, and so forth), the materials used to construct your home (brick, stucco, and so on), the type of roof on your home (wood, composition shingles, tile, etc.), the age of your home (new or old), the type and number of rooms in your home (one bathroom or many), the safety features in your home (smoke alarms, sprinklers, etc.), plus much more. If something is part of your home, it will generally impact either positively or negatively the cost of insuring it.

Location of Your Home—Homes in different locations can be subject to different risks. For example, your home might be in an area where there has been a rash of thefts or wildfires, or in a location subject to hurricanes. How close your home is to a fire department and/or fire hydrants also plays a role.

Extra or Supplemental Coverage—If you select extra coverage to increase or extend the amount of coverage in your policy or buy additional coverage that is not part of your standard policy, it will affect the amount of your premium.

plain talk

A premium is the amount paid to an insurance company in exchange for insurance coverage for a specific period of time.

Amount of Your Deductible—Your deductible is the amount you pay out of pocket before your insurance kicks in. A higher deductible can help lower your premiums, if you are willing and able to cover the smaller losses yourself.

Your Claims History—If you have submitted homeowner's insurance claims in the past, it can affect the cost of your coverage and even your ability to get coverage in the future. Remember, insurance is to protect you against the big losses you can't handle on your own, not the smaller ones you can manage.

Your Credit Information—Your credit history and insurance history can sometimes be used by insurance companies as an indicator of how likely you will be to file a claim. This is yet another reason to keep your credit history clean.

Saving Money

I t is possible to maintain an adequate level of insurance coverage and still save money on homeowner's insurance. Discounts are available for a wide variety of reasons. Here are some factors that may help you to save on your insurance premiums.

Deductibles—A higher deductible can lower your premium. By assuming more of the risk yourself, you may be able to lower your premium and avoid filing claims for small losses. Remember, you will have to pay for any losses up to the amount of your deductible, so make sure your deductible is at a level you can afford to cover.

Safety Measures—Improving or increasing the safety and security of your home may make you eligible for discounts. Installing dead bolts, window locks, or central alarm systems (burglar alarms and smoke detectors) can trigger dis-

smart step

Be sure to include the amount of your deductible when determining how much money to set aside for an emergency fund.

smart step

Conduct a thorough inventory of your personal property to help you determine an adequate amount of insurance coverage to protect your interests.

counts because they help to prevent losses. Plus, they can be a great idea for your peace of mind.

Coverage Amounts—You need enough coverage for the structure, your personal property, and personal liability. Make sure it is both adequate and appropriate for your needs, but do not overinsure. One common mistake is to include the value of the land under your home in the coverage amount.

Comparing Quotations—It is always a good idea to compare costs and to shop around to lower your expenses, but don't focus only on price. Make sure that you are getting good value, too. While you are checking prices, also look for service and dependability of both your insurance professional and the company.

Multiple Policy Discounts—If you choose to purchase your insurance coverage for both your home and automobile from one company, you may receive a discount on one, the other, or both policies. It will also make it easier for your insurance professional to identify any gaps in your coverage.

Miscellaneous Discounts—There are a variety of other discounts that your insurance company may offer. They can include discounts for having a new home, not smoking, being a senior citizen, or staying with the company for a long time. Check with your insurance professional for details.

Group Coverage—Your employer, labor union, or alumni association or a similar group may offer a group discount for their employees or members.

Policy Review—Insurance needs change over time. At least once a year, review your insurance needs with your insurance professional. You may find that you need more or less coverage than the year before. If you need more, you can purchase additional protection; if you need less, you can modify your coverage. Either way, you should be certain you have adequate protection.

THE CHALLENGE

When Gene bought his home, he didn't give much thought to the homeowner's insurance policy he needed to close on the home. He contacted a company that he heard had low rates (money was tight at closing) and bought a standard policy. After a few years, with his premium increasing annually, Gene thought he needed a change. He tried to contact the company to find out why his rates kept going up, but he could never get anyone to take his calls. He heard that the company had lost a lot of money covering tornado claims in the Midwest, and he believed they were trying to make it up by increasing homeowners' rates across the board. Gene was determined to find a better deal, but he wasn't sure where to start.

THE PLAN

Gene's first step is to discuss his situation with Christine, the insurance professional who now handles his automobile insurance. Christine evaluates Gene's coverage and notices that he is not adequately insured because the amount of coverage he had originally purchased was only for the amount of the mortgage. In addition, he had chosen not to purchase replacement cost coverage. If something had happened to his home, he probably wouldn't have had enough money to rebuild. Gene was shocked. "I thought I was covered, but I guess I really wasn't," he stated.

Christine asks Gene to do a complete inventory of his home. Then she and Gene review the inventory and look around the home to make sure he hasn't missed any major items that might need coverage and to make sure he would receive all the discounts to which he was entitled. After reviewing the options with Gene, Christine explains that Gene can purchase replacement cost coverage and qualify for additional discounts by installing a security system, dead bolts, and window locks and by insuring his home and automobile with the same company.

With the discounts Gene receives, the cost of his coverage is about the same as the cost of his previous policy, but his coverage is better. Christine suggests that they get together on an annual basis to make sure his needs haven't changed. "My goal was to save money on my insurance, but I feel better now knowing that I am covered if something happens," added Gene.

smart step

Start Now!

Determine
how much you
should set aside
for emergencies.

Log on to
hrblock.com/advisor

Keeping a Record

You need to create a home inventory so if you ever need to make a claim, you will be prepared. Begin by walking through your home, ideally with a video camera, although a still camera, or even a pad and pen, will do. Document anything worth more than $50. Work methodically, room by room. Open the closets, dressers, cabinets, and drawers. Don't worry about the mess; what you are doing is making a record of everything you have. Make sure you document possessions in the attic, basement, shed, and garage. Include all jewelry, clothing, collections, CDs, tools, electronic equipment, and other valuables.

Your inventory should also document how old each item is, its make and model (if applicable), receipts, owner's manuals, purchase price, and so on. For difficult-to-price items (such as collectibles), you may need a professional appraisal. After you make your inventory, store it in a safe and secure place, such as a safe deposit box or a fireproof safe.

In the event that your home *is* damaged or destroyed by fire or some other disaster, or if your home is burgled, what do you do?

Of course, you will need to promptly call the authorities (police or fire department), if necessary, and your insurance professional. If there is damage, make temporary repairs (such as covering a broken window) to help prevent any further damage. Be sure to keep your receipts for any temporary repairs. Take photos and make a list of the damage. When the insurance company's claims adjuster inspects the damage, be there if at all possible. You increase your chances of getting a proper settlement if you are prepared with the documentation to back up your claim. Have the inventory you prepared handy and write down names, dates, and who said what. Keeping good notes and records both before and after a loss will make the process go more smoothly.

Should you have a covered loss, don't panic. You have insurance to protect you from loss. The reason you bought your homeowner's insurance policy was to make sure your financial interests relating to your home were protected. Don't be afraid to ask for help from your insurance professional—that is what he or she is there for!

the ESSENTIALS

1 Lenders require adequate coverage to protect their interests (the amount of the mortgage), but you should opt for adequate coverage for your interests (structure, personal property, personal liability).

2 Homeowner's policies are similar, but they vary in the type and level of coverage. Determine what type of policy best meets your needs.

3 Exclusions to your homeowner's policy will indicate perils (specific causes of loss or damage) that are not covered.

4 There are many ways to save money on your homeowner's insurance. Don't sacrifice coverage you may need to save on the amount of your premium.

5 To be prepared in the event of a claim, keep good records and make an inventory of your personal property.

smart step

When you've made the decision to purchase a home, review your life insurance coverage. The amount of your mortgage could be another factor that impacts your need for coverage or the level of coverage you already have.

12

THE JOYS OF HOME OWNERSHIP:
Maintaining Your Investment

"We shape our dwellings and afterward they shape us."
—Winston Churchill

Start Now!

Calculate the
value of making
extra principal
payments.

Log on to
hrblock.com/advisor

A home is often the biggest investment most people will make in their lives, and maintaining that investment takes both time and money. But maintaining a home is well worth the effort. By caring for your home, and factoring in some annual appreciation, your investment should grow over the years, while providing you with a place to live at the same time. Maintaining your investment, both financially and physically, ensures that you will have a home to be proud of for years to come.

Maintaining your home financially includes paying the mortgage in full and on time, refinancing if appropriate, paying property taxes, and maintaining adequate insurance on your home. Maintaining your home physically includes performing preventive maintenance, repairs, and remodeling should your home need some changes now or in the future. You've done all the work necessary to find and purchase your home, so it makes sense that you'll want to take good care of it.

Mortgage Payments

Maintaining your property means making your mortgage payments on time. A short time after you settle into your new home, you will receive from your lender a set of coupons (unless your lender sends you a monthly statement) with which to pay your mortgage. It is important that you use these coupons when making your mortgage payment because they allow the lender to properly apply your payment to your loan. If you don't have the coupon, be sure to write your loan number on the memo section of your check when you remit payment.

It is unlikely you will keep the same mortgage for the entire term of your original loan (due to refinancing, loan sales, etc.), but you will nevertheless be making that payment for many years. As you make those payments, you are paying a great deal of interest as well as principal. In this section, we will show you how, with just a little effort, you may be able to drastically reduce the overall cost of your loan.

Paying It Off Faster

Just because you sign a 30-year mortgage doesn't mean you have to make monthly payments for the next thirty years. There are ways to expedite the process, particularly if your personal financial picture brightens. Here are a few ways to pay off your loan faster, and save thousands of dollars in interest payments in the process.

Shorten the Term of Your Mortgage—If your income increases, you may be able to afford higher monthly payments. You might think that you would pay twice as much each month for a 15-year mortgage as you would for a 30-year, because you pay it off twice as fast, but the difference is not nearly as great as you might expect. Generally, you can get a slightly better interest rate on a 15-year mortgage. If interest rates drop after you get your first mortgage, you'll do even better. On a $150,000 mortgage, if your choice is between a 15-year mortgage at 7 percent and a 30-year mortgage at 7.25 percent, you would pay about $1,350 (principal and interest—P&I) a month on the 15-year and about $1,025 (P&I) per month on the 30-year. Over the course of the mortgage, you would make total mortgage payments of about $369,000 on the 30-year (including approximately $218,400 in interest), and about $243,000 on the 15-year (including approximately $92,700 in interest). That's a savings of $125,700 of interest on a $150,000 mortgage. That's why so many homebuyers are willing to pay the extra $200 to $300 a month to fund a 15-year mortgage.

Add a Lump Sum—If you get a bonus or an inheritance or save a large amount of money, you might consider using it to pay down some of the principal on your loan. That can shorten the term dramatically. For instance, on a 30-year,

smart step

If you've been deducting points over the life of a mortgage and you refinance that mortgage, you can deduct any points not previously deducted in the year of refinancing.

7 percent, $150,000 mortgage, if you pay an additional $20,000 after five years, you could cut the mortgage term down by about seven years and save you approximately $67,920 of interest. Before you send in a lump sum, make sure your loan does not contain any prepayment penalties, which are fees some lenders charge for paying a loan before it is due.

Make Extra Principal Payments—If you make additional monthly payments, you will experience a decrease in the mortgage term and the total interest. For instance, if you are scheduled to pay $998 (P&I) per month on a $150,000, 30-year, 7 percent mortgage, add another $200 if possible for a $1,198 monthly payment. That extra $200 per month will pay off the loan about eleven years faster and save you approximately $89,276 of interest. Again, check the terms of your loan for any prepayment penalties that may apply.

Another popular way to pay off a mortgage faster is by making biweekly payments. Instead of making your payment once a month, you make half your monthly payment every two weeks. There are fifty-two weeks in a year, so you would end up making twenty-six half payments, which would equal thirteen monthly payments, or one additional payment more than you would have normally made during the year. The payments would be applied more quickly to your loan balance, serving to decrease both the mortgage term and the total interest paid.

Some lenders or third-party payment companies may charge you a fee to process this type of payment arrangement, but you can accomplish approximately the same thing on your own. Simply divide the amount of your monthly payment (principal and interest) by twelve and add that amount to your normal monthly payment each month indicating that it is for an additional principal payment. By the end of the year, you'll have made that additional monthly payment and shaved off some time and interest from your loan. For instance, if you are scheduled to pay $998 (P&I) a month on a $150,000, 30-year, 7 percent

CONVENTIONAL PAYMENTS VERSUS ACCELERATED PAYMENTS		
	CONVENTIONAL PAYMENTS	**ACCELERATED PAYMENTS**
Loan amount	$150,000	$150,000
Monthly payment (principal and interest only)	$998	$1,081
Additional monthly principal payment amount (included above)*	$0	$83
Loan interest rate	7%	7%
Loan term	30 years	Approximately 24 years
Total interest paid	$209,263	$158,123
Total savings:		
Term of loan	0 years	6.2 years sooner
Intere st	$0	$51,140

*Example assumes that additional payment is made each month.

smart step

Start Now!

Calculate whether or not it makes sense financially for you to refinance.

Log on to

hrblock.com/advisor

mortgage, add another $83 ($998 divided by twelve months) for a $1,081 monthly payment. That extra $83 per month will pay off the loan about six years faster and save you approximately $51,140 of interest. Again, check the terms of your loan for any prepayment penalties that may apply.

Refinance—If interest rates drop enough, you might be able to get a new mortgage with better rates. You may have to pay extra points to refinance, but a better interest rate will generally make it worthwhile in the long run, particularly if you stay in the home for several more years. For instance, if you're paying off a $150,000 loan at 8 percent for thirty years, you would be paying about $1,100 per month (P&I). If you refinanced at 6 percent, you would be able to pay the loan off about eleven years sooner with the same monthly payment or reduce your monthly payment to about $899 a month if you held to the 30-year

See your tax pro-
fessional before
you take out a
home equity
loan or establish
a line of credit
secured by your
home. He or she
can help you
determine what
portion of your
interest payments
will be deductible.

term. There is hidden money in your home, and refinancing at a lower interest rate is one way to get it out.

Should you refinance? The decision depends upon a variety of factors such as how long you intend to stay in your home, what the difference is in interest rates, and how much it will cost you to refinance. If you plan to stay in your home for several years and there is more than a 2 percent difference between your current rate and the going rate, you should probably consider refinancing. Also consider whether or not you have the money needed for closing costs. FHA and VA loans allow you to add certain closing costs to a refinancing package, but you will still need to have some cash to close the new loan. For refinancing to make sense financially, you must be able to recoup the costs associated with refinancing.

Using the Equity in Your Home

The best reason to apply for a new mortgage is that interest rates have dropped enough so you will realize significant savings. But there are other ways to use the equity in your home. As you continue to pay your mortgage every month, and as your home appreciates, your equity grows. It's like money in the bank. A home equity loan allows you to tap the equity in your home and use it for other purposes. What can you do with your home equity? Many things, so consider these options:

■ **Consolidate your consumer debts and roll them into your mortgage.**
You can eliminate your consumer debt, lower your total monthly payments, and often get a tax deduction for all your interest paid because the mortgage is secured by your home. The main problem with this strategy is that if you don't change your spending habits, you could end up in worse shape and put your home in jeopardy. It may make more sense to stop running up more consumer debt.

- **Switch from an adjustable-rate mortgage to a fixed-rate mortgage.** Locking in a fixed rate protects you from possible future interest rate increases.
- **Cancel private mortgage insurance when you have built up enough equity and are no longer required to pay that extra money.** Your lender may not automatically stop charging you for mortgage insurance, so you need to act on it yourself. The savings are well worth the effort.
- **Pay for college tuition, home improvements, a car, or some other major purchase.** You can also use your equity to finance a new business. If you need money, your home can help you get it.
- **Get a home equity loan or line of credit.** You don't have to get a new mortgage to use the equity in your home to generate cash. There are other ways to tap into the equity, including:
- **Home equity loan.** You can get a home equity loan, using your home as collateral. The interest you pay is often tax deductible, and it may be cheaper to get a home equity loan than a new mortgage. Although the interest rate may be higher on the home equity loan, lenders may not charge some of the fees on home equity loans that they do on new mortgages. A home equity loan reduces the amount of equity you have in the home.
- **Home equity line of credit.** This allows you to borrow against home equity as needed using a checkbook or credit card. With a line of credit, you borrow only what you need when you need it, and you pay it back according to the terms of your line of credit. Once you have repaid the loan, you can use the line of credit again for something else, and you can keep tapping into it with no closing costs and no new application procedure as long as you have the line of credit. The danger is that a line of credit can lead some consumers to over-spend, just like credit cards can.

Reverse Mortgage—If you have paid off all or most of your mortgage, you may be able to use a reverse mortgage to generate monthly income from your home equity. Instead of paying the lender, the lender pays you. Typically, a reverse mortgage pays you a lump sum, fixed monthly payments, a line of credit,

fast fact

Rolling debt into your home puts your home at risk if you default on the loan. Be sure you can pay off the new loan before you put your home at risk.

or a combination of these. The loan is due when the home is no longer your principal residence—if you sell the home, move out permanently, or die. The home doesn't have to be sold to pay off the loan, but if it is, any proceeds in excess of the amount owed on the reverse mortgage is paid to you or your estate. Reverse mortgage payments aren't taxed, so they don't reduce Social Security and Medicare benefits. The most popular reverse mortgage programs are sponsored by Fannie Mae and require the homeowner to be at least sixty-two years old. There are three primary programs:

- **Home Keeper.** This basic program allows you to borrow against the equity in your home. A lender that participates in the program pays you equal monthly payments that continue until the loan is due, allows you to tap a line of credit, or a combination of both. You repay the loan when you sell the home or no longer use it as your principal residence or your estate pays it when you die. Repayment of the loan will include interest and other financing costs.

- **Home Keeper for Home Purchase.** You can buy a new home with a reverse mortgage loan. You make a down payment as you would normally, but you won't have monthly payments. You take out a reverse mortgage for the balance and the home acts as security for the reverse mortgage, which you or your estate repays when you sell or otherwise permanently leave the home.

- **Home Equity Conversion Mortgage.** This is similar to a Home Keeper mortgage, but with two additional payment options. In addition to monthly payments for as long as you occupy the home as a principal residence, a line of credit, or a combination of the two, additional payment options also include monthly payments for a specified term or monthly payments for a term combined with a line of credit.

There are many reasons why you might want to tap the equity in your home. The loans often make sense, but a few words of caution are in order. First, beware of home equity loans that offer more than 100 percent of your equity. For example, if your equity is $100,000 in the home (worth $150,000), and you received an offer for 120 percent of your equity, the loan would be for $120,000. That number may sound enticing, but taking on a loan of that size means you will owe more than the home is worth, which is not a good idea. Being **upside down** on a home makes it almost impossible to sell the property, because you would have to sell the home for $20,000 more than it is worth to pay off your loans (the original loan plus the home equity loan).

Second, be careful when using home equity to pay off credit cards. Credit cards are unsecured debt, which means there is no collateral attached to the debt. But a home loan is a secured debt, and the home secures the debt. When you use home equity to pay off credit cards, you are trading unsecured debt for secured debt, and that may not be smart. Why? Because if you fail to pay your unsecured credit cards, you will probably ruin your credit rating, but if you fail to pay a secured home loan, you lose your home. It's usually not a smart trade.

Paying Property Taxes

Another financial item to consider is your property taxes. Understanding your property taxes and the options you may have allows you to make intelligent financial choices. If you don't understand how much you have to pay, when or how to pay it, or how to budget appropriately, property taxes can get out of hand and put both your investment and your place to live at risk.

There are two ways to pay your property taxes: You can pay them out of an impound account, or you can pay them directly when they are due. As we discussed in Chapter 10, lenders sometimes require borrowers to open an impound account to prepay taxes and insurance. Let's take a closer look at paying your taxes via this option.

plain talk

When you owe more than the property is worth, it is called being upside down.

Paying property tax payments from impound accounts works this way: You pay an initial amount into the account at closing, and you add to that account on a monthly basis with a portion of your monthly payment. When the tax payment is due, the lender pays the taxes from this account. The amount of the initial deposit depends upon when your taxes are payable and the amount of **cushion** the lender requires to ensure there will be adequate funds in the account to pay the bills when they come due. Typically, if taxes are due within six months of closing of escrow, you may have to pay six or more months of taxes into the impound account at closing. On the other hand, if the previous owner has paid the taxes through the close of escrow, your initial account could be as little as three months worth of taxes.

If your lender does not require an impound account or if you opt to pay your taxes directly, you control your money until the bill is due. You are also responsible for making sure the bill is actually paid. Generally speaking, homeowners are assessed property taxes once a year and have a couple of months to pay the bill after they receive it. If, for example, your tax bill arrives on November 15, you might have until December 31 to pay it before penalties are added. Most homeowners pay their property taxes before December 31, so they can claim a deduction when filing their federal income taxes.

County tax assessors usually offer a few payment options to taxpayers:

- **If you pay early, you might be eligible for an early-bird discount.**
- **If you can't pay your taxes in full, or if you are billed once a year and you find the bill is too much to pay all at once, you may be able to arrange quarterly payments.**
- **If you can't pay in full, partial payments may be accepted** (although the delinquency will accrue interest and penalties).
- **Credit card payments and online bill payment are usually options.**

Not Paying Property Taxes

Most of us would rather not pay taxes, but not paying property taxes is not an option. Not paying taxes will result in a number of significant problems, all of which can be avoided by paying your taxes in a timely manner. The longer taxes are delinquent, the more expensive the problems become, including:

Penalties and Interest—When taxes are not paid in a timely manner, penalties and interest charges may be added to the bill. So on top of your regular tax bill, you will have to pay penalty and interest on the outstanding bill, which is generally added on a monthly basis.

Tax Lien—If your taxes remain unpaid, a tax lien may be filed against your property. The lien gives the government the power to foreclose and seize your real estate, which can then be auctioned to the highest bidder with the proceeds being used to pay your tax bill.

Sale of the Property—If a tax lien is placed upon your property, it will cloud the title. Remember, a clouded title has a dispute attached to it, such as a lien. A clouded title will render the sale all but impossible. If a **lis pendens** (lien) is filed against a property because of the owner's failure to pay the property taxes, there are three ways to avoid a foreclosure:

1. **Pay the taxes.**
2. **Prove that the property is not subject to the tax.** (For example, show that a church, school, or other nonprofit group owns it.)
3. **File bankruptcy** (although doing so does not relieve the owner of the obligation of paying the taxes.)

plain talk

A lis pendens is the name of a legal notice recorded against a property stating that there is a lien against it.

Reducing Your Tax Bill

Property taxes are based on the **assessed value** of your home. The assessed value is multiplied by the local tax rate, and that is what you owe. For example, if the tax rate is $10 per $1,000 assessed value, and if your home is assessed at $175,000, your property taxes would be $1,750 per year.

Although your search and comparison of homes should have given you a good idea of how much your tax bill is going to be, your first tax assessment or tax bill may be a shock. A bill for several thousand dollars usually is. Is it possible to reduce your tax bill? It may be, but to do so you must prove that the assessment of your property is incorrect.

If your tax bill seems unusually large, it may be that the tax assessor's office made a mistake. Perhaps local comparable homes were not used correctly, or someone made a clerical error, or there are problems with your particular property, or the market is changing. A number of reasons can result in your property being valued incorrectly. If the valuation is incorrect, then the assessed tax will be incorrect as well. To reduce your taxes, you must prove to the assessor that your home is worth less than the originally assessed value or that there is a mistake in your property's assessment.

Keep in mind that proving this can be counterproductive. You will be arguing that your home isn't worth as much as the assessor says it is. Arguing that your home isn't as valuable as the taxman says is like telling the guy who is buying your car that he should not offer as much for it. This argument can affect the sales price of your home when and if you decide to sell it, because buyers and sellers often look at assessed value as a starting point to determine the value of a home.

plain talk

The assessed value of a home is the value placed upon it for tax purposes. It may or may not be the same as market value or appraised value.

If you decide to challenge your assessment, you must file an appeal with the assessor's office. To be successful, you will have to prove that what you are saying is correct and that the assessed valuation is wrong. Here are some factors affecting home valuation:

- **Your home appraisal.** Obtain an independent expert opinion of the actual market value of your home. A complete and thorough analysis of the home will help establish its value.
- **Sales of comparable homes.** Sales of comparable homes in your neighborhood can help establish value. Remember, they need to be comparable homes, so they should be similar in size, age, location, and so forth. The information you compile on homes used for comparison should include addresses, sales prices and dates, photographs, as well as any other specifics your local assessor may require.
- **Proof of problems.** If there is a problem with your home that is not evident, you must submit proof of its existence. You must also supply estimates for repairs from contractors and photographs of the problems to help document your claim.

Insurance Reviews

Insurance needs change over time. At any point after setting up your homeowner's insurance, you may need more coverage or you may need less. So at least once a year, you should give yourself an insurance checkup. Here are a few areas to consider:

Private Mortgage Insurance (PMI)—This insurance is not a part of your insurance coverage, but if you are paying PMI as part of your monthly mortgage payment, you should review it once a year. The Homeowner's Protection Act of 1998 established rules for the automatic termination of PMI on home mortgages. Under this federal law, your PMI should be canceled once you have 20

fast fact

Filing an appeal does not relieve you of the obligation to pay your tax bill.

percent equity in your home based on the original property value. If you find that you have built up 20 percent or more equity in your home and your PMI has not been cancelled, contact your lender.

Homeowner's Insurance—As time goes by, your need for the different types and levels of homeowner's coverage can change. You and your insurance professional should meet once a year to review your coverage to ensure it is adequate and appropriate for your needs. You may find that you have additional items that need to be covered or coverage that you no longer need. Either way, you'll want to be sure your coverage is right for you.

If your initial policy did not include replacement cost coverage, you should probably consider including it now. Look for coverage that provides for the full cost of replacing your home and its contents should disaster strike. It is never too late to change, and it is always smart to do so. If you need to cut expenses, consider other alternatives such as increasing your deductible. You don't want to be caught short if you experience a loss.

If you have acquired any valuable items, such as jewelry or antiques, you may need to obtain a **rider** to insure these items. Without a rider, your homeowner's policy may not provide coverage or may provide only a limited amount of coverage for valuable items such as these. If you have started a business that you operate out of your home or have a home office, you may need to obtain coverage, because most homeowner's insurance policies do not cover business property.

Maintaining your home involves more than just physically caring for it. It requires that you make intelligent financial choices along the way. Too many homeowners purchase an insurance policy, renew it every year, and don't ever take the time to update it. That could be a costly mistake. Schedule an appointment with your insurance professional at least annually to review your coverage so you are sure it is adequate.

Home Maintenance

Your home and land must be maintained if your investment is to bring you the maximum financial and emotional return. A regular program of preventive maintenance can avert big problems. For example, by tending to a roofing issue when it first occurs, you may prevent the need for a complete overhaul down the road. Even if you are not handy, it is important to monitor your home. Preventive maintenance is not difficult to learn and, again, can save you a lot of time and money.

What do you need to monitor, and how often? It has been said that you can learn something every day if you just keep your eyes open, and that applies to your home as well. Look around and be observant every day so you can catch the small things before they turn into big things. On the following page is a checklist of items you may want to consider when looking around and checking out your home. Your home may call for you to add some items or check some items more or less frequently, but this list should give you an idea of where to start.

Making Repairs

Sooner or later, something will break and you will need to make repairs to your home. Some things are easy to fix, even for the novice, such as changing a light bulb, while others are not, such as rewiring an electrical circuit. So the first thing to consider is whether or not you can and want to tackle a particular repair.

If you decide to tackle the repair yourself, remember that some repairs around the home can be dangerous, such as those repairs involving gas or electricity. Also keep in mind that if you attempt a repair and find you cannot complete it, hiring a professional to finish the repair will probably take more time and cost even more. So remember the motto When in doubt, farm it out!

smart step

Hiring a professional contractor can be expensive. But consider your skill level and the value of your time when deciding whether or not to do it yourself.

HOME MAINTENANCE CHECKLIST		
ITEM TO BE CHECKED	EVERY MONTH	EVERY 6 MONTHS
EXTERIOR		
Look around whenever you're outside. If you see something suspicious, check it out.	✓	
Chimneys and fireplaces: Inspect for proper operation and obstructions.		✓
Doors and windows: Check operation and caulking.		✓
Driveway and sidewalks: Check for deterioration and cracks.		✓
Gutters and downspouts: Clean out any debris.		✓
Heating and air-conditioning: Make sure exterior unit is free from obstructions and service if necessary.		✓
Lawn: Remove any debris and check for hazards.	✓	
Pools and spas: Check for proper operation and look for safety hazards.	✓	
Roof: Check for deterioration, including missing or broken shingles and leakage.		✓
Walls and siding: Inspect all surfaces for deterioration, including mold, rot, chipping paint, or warping.		✓
INTERIOR		
Look around whenever you're inside. If you see something suspicious, check it out.	✓	
Appliances: Check for proper operation.	✓	
Attic: Check for leaks, pests, and damage.		✓
Basement: Check for leaks, cracks, mold, pests, and safety hazards.		✓
Bathrooms: Check for leaks and look for safety hazards.	✓	
Electrical: Trip main circuit breaker and check ground fault interrupters (GFI).		✓
Kitchen: Check for leaks and look for safety hazards.	✓	
Heating and air-conditioning: Change filter monthly and service if necessary.	✓	
Plumbing: Check for leaks.		✓
Smoke detectors and alarm systems: Check operation and replace batteries twice a year.		✓
Water heater: Check for leaks, test pressure relief valve, and flush as specified.		✓

E CHALLENGE

k, Sue, and their two children, Beth and Belle, have lived in their home for several years. One
ue notices that the water coming out of the kitchen sink and the shower doesn't seem to have
pressure. To make matters worse, Sue runs out of hot water when she fills the whirlpool tub.
ank decides to investigate the problem. The plumbing looks fine on the surface but when he re-
ves the aerator from the faucet and the showerhead from the shower, he finds they are clogged
h small white particles that appear to be plastic or some sort of mineral deposit. Hank decides to
investigate further. He describes his problem to a few local plumbers who tell him it sounds like a "dip
tube" problem with the hot water heater, which will probably need to be replaced. In addition, the fixtures should be cleaned and the hot water lines flushed. It appears that Hank has an expensive problem to fix. The question is, can he fix it himself or will he need to call in a professional?

THE PLAN

Hank decides he needs more information to determine if what the plumbers have told him was correct.
He goes online and finds that the make and model
number of his hot water heater has been included in
a class-action. The lawsuit describes a defect in the
part that carries cold water into the heater. It is disin-
tegrating and clogging the fixtures. Unfortunately,
Hank also finds that time has run out for filing a claim,
so he will have to pay for a new hot water heater.

Hank's final decision was whether or not he can
tackle the installation himself. Hank is handy and the
repair seems straightforward, but it also includes
hooking up the natural gas connection. Hank doesn't
want to make an error and end up with a potentially
explosive situation. So he makes a second round of
calls for quotes on purchasing and installing a new
hot water heater. Many of the quotes include disposal
of the old unit. Hank hates to spend the extra money
for something he can do himself, but he is busy and
doesn't have a lot of spare time. It is a tough decision.

In the end, Hank decides to have the hot water
heater professionally installed. It costs more, but
Hank decides the time he spends with his family is
more valuable than the expense. Moreover, he will
be sure that his hot water heater is installed properly
and meets all local building codes. "The larger tank
should give us plenty of hot water," Hank said. "And
I hope it will keep me out of hot water with my family at the same time."

187

smart step

Don't wait until an addition is completed before notifying your insurance professional. Review your coverage needs before you begin remodeling.

There is nothing wrong with calling an expert in the beginning. Doing so will probably save you time and aggravation, if not money. But it is always a good idea to learn new things. Owning a home is more expensive if you have to call an expert every time something goes wrong. So as with many other things, it will pay to learn about home repair so you can handle some repairs and be an informed consumer when you need to call the professionals.

Remodeling

The longer you live in a home, the more you will notice what you like and don't like and what you want to or need to change. Needs change, children grow up, styles evolve, but the home remains the same. That is, of course, until you remodel. Remodeling can help you in several ways. First, you get to change your home to better fit your needs, and, second, that change may serve to increase the value of the home. You may even be able to get more for your home when the time comes to sell.

As far as resale value goes, all home remodeling projects are not created equal. Some can add value to your home, while others may actually make your home less desirable to potential buyers. Generally speaking, projects that update or improve the home, such as a kitchen or bath remodel, or add living space, such as that additional bedroom, will add value to the home. Projects that add amenities to your home, such as a pool, may add value for some potential buyers, but they may subtract value for others who may be concerned about upkeep, maintenance, or safety. Resale value is certainly a factor to consider, and you should be sure your project makes sense for your situation both now and in the future.

Everyone has probably heard at least one horror story about a remodeling job. There is one truism about remodeling: It always costs more and takes longer than you anticipated. But that does not mean it has to cost a lot more and take a lot longer. There are two ways to keep your remodeling costs in check. First, know exactly what you want. Get magazines, attend seminars at your local home improvement store, and read up. Knowing what you want will allow less room for error.

Second, find a contractor with a sterling reputation. Ask around, call some companies, check references, and make sure the person you are hiring is good.

✓ Interviewing a Contractor

- **Experience**—How long has the contractor been in business? Your contractor should be experienced in your type of remodeling project. Find out how many projects like yours he or she has completed.

- **Licensing**—Your contractor should have the proper licenses to conduct business in your area.

- **References**—Your contractor should easily provide references and contact information. Check the references and look for a contractor with satisfied customers.

- **Guarantee**—Does your contractor offer a guarantee? If so, what does it cover and for how long? If not, why not?

- **Insurance**—Your contractor should be properly insured. Liability insurance protects your property and worker compensation insurance protects you from liability if a worker is injured during the project. Find out who provides this coverage and if there have been any claims.

- **Permits**—Your contractor should obtain permits and complete the work according to local building codes.

- **Supervision**—Who performs the work? Does the contractor do it? Or is it delegated to a subcontractor? Who supervises the work?

- **Memberships**—Does the contractor belong to any professional associations, such as the National Association of Home Builders (NAHB) or the National Association of the Remodeling Industry (NARI)?

A home is a major investment and needs to be treated as such. Caring for it, both financially and physically, is the best way to protect the investment that is your home. If you take care of your home, when the time comes to sell, it will probably take care of you, too.

the ESSENTIALS

1 Paying your mortgage payment every two weeks instead of once a month can save you money by reducing the amount of interest you will pay over the lifetime of the loan.

2 Refinancing can be a smart option. A lower interest rate or shorter-term loan can save you money over the life of the loan.

3 Not paying property taxes can lead to many problems. If you think the assessment on your home is too high, you can file an appeal.

4 Review your insurance coverage yearly to make sure your coverage is up to date.

5 Preventive maintenance helps protect your investment and helps your home's value grow. Don't be afraid to call in a professional if necessary.

13 [Home Buying Matters:
Frequently Asked Home Buying
Questions and Answers]

"The important thing is not to stop questioning."
—Albert Einstein

Buying a home is a complex process. There are many decisions to be made along the way, including determining if home ownership is right for you. Where and what should you buy? How should you finance the purchase? What insurance coverage do you need? What are the taxes going to cost? We have covered many topics, but it is hard to include everything in one book. Following are commonly asked questions, organized alphabetically on home buying topics from contracts to taxes and more.

Contracts

Q. The contract and paperwork for the purchase of my home seem very complicated. Do I need to hire a lawyer?

A. It depends on the state. Some states require that you hire a lawyer, but many do not. Call the state's Department of Real Estate to find out the rules. But if you are not required to have a lawyer, consider hiring one anyway. A real estate contract is not easy to understand, and a good lawyer can help you understand it and assist you in getting the best deal.

Q. We made an offer on a home and it was accepted. Now we are feeling that it wasn't the right decision. Can we back out of the contract?

A. Probably not. Unless there is a contingency that hasn't been met, your contract mandates that you buy the house. If you back out now, the owner could sue you and win.

Credit

Q. What can we do now, before we apply, to ensure that we qualify for a mortgage loan?

A. Your first step should be to check your credit report. Make sure it is accurate before you apply for a loan. If it isn't or if you need to get it cleaned up, do so before you apply for a loan. Next, consider activities you should *avoid* if you are thinking of applying for a loan. Avoid taking on any additional debt, such as a car loan, because the debt will impact your debt ratio. Be careful when transferring funds and opening or closing accounts. When you provide documentation of the source of your funds, movement between or among accounts can be confusing or appear unusual.

Q. I found an error on my credit report. What should I do?

A. You need to dispute the mistake and make sure it is corrected. Send proof that the item is incorrect to the appropriate credit-reporting bureau and follow up to make sure your credit history is corrected. By law, the bureau has to correct the error. Remember there are three major credit-reporting bureaus, not just one. That same error may show up on all three credit reports, or there may be different errors on your other credit reports. Get copies of your credit report from all three companies. You can also obtain a 3-in-1 report that merges reports from the three bureaus. It is wise to routinely check your credit records (at least annually) for accuracy and especially before you apply for a loan.

- **Equifax** (800-685-1111 or www.equifax.com)
- **Experian** (888-397-3742 or www.experian.com)
- **TransUnion** (800-888-4213 or www.transunion.com)

Discrimination

Q. My husband and I feel that our real estate agent is showing us homes in only certain areas, even though we have expressed interest in other neighborhoods. What should we do?

A. If you feel your real estate agent is steering you toward or away from certain neighborhoods because of your race, color, religion, sex, nationality, family status, or disability, you should contact the Office of Fair Housing in the U.S. Department of Housing and Urban Development (HUD) at 800-669-9777 or online at www.hud.gov. The Fair Housing Act prohibits discrimination in almost all housing-related transactions, including selling or financing a home.

Q. I made an offer on a house and it wasn't accepted. I think it was because of my race. Sellers can't discriminate against me, can they?

A. No, they cannot. In fact, there are numerous fair housing laws that protect people from housing discrimination:

- **The Fair Housing Act**—Title VIII of the Civil Rights Act of 1968 (The Fair Housing Act) prohibits discrimination in the sale, rental, and financing of homes on the basis of race, color, national origin, religion, sex, pregnancy, familial status (including having children under the age of 18), and disability.
- **The Civil Rights Act of 1964**—Title VI prohibits discrimination on the basis of race, color, or national origin by anyone involved with a program that receives federal funds, including organizations that use HUD and FHA loans, as well as any business that works with the government.
- **The Americans with Disabilities Act of 1990**— Among other things, this act prohibits housing discrimination against people with disabilities.
- **The Age Discrimination Act of 1975**—This act effectively prohibits discrimination on the basis of age.

If you feel that you have been the victim of housing discrimination, you should probably contact your lawyer.

Home Buying

Q. My wife and I think we are ready to buy a home. How do we know if home ownership is right for us?

A. If you answer *yes* to the following questions, you may be ready to consider buying a home:

- Do you plan to live in the same area for several years?
- Do you have a steady income that will enable you to make mortgage payments for the next fifteen to thirty years?
- Do you have the extra time and money to maintain a home?
- Do you have the money to cover the down payment?
- Do you have a credit rating solid enough to qualify for a mortgage?

If you answered *yes* to all five questions, then you're probably ready to consider buying a home.

Q. Is there a perfect time to buy a home?

A. No, and you should be wary of falling into the trap created by that sort of thinking. Waiting for interest rates to fall a little more, or the market to soften up a bit, or the price of the home to drop is usually a mistake. The home you love will probably be gone. The right time to buy a home is when you find the home that is right for you, you can afford it, and you want to purchase it.

Q. Is there anything I can do to ensure that my home will be a sound investment?

A. That well-worn phrase of real estate professionals—Location, location, location—is a favorite for a reason. If you have a choice, it is almost always better to buy a lesser house in a better neighborhood than a better house in a lesser neighborhood. You can always spruce the house up, but you can't spruce up an entire neighborhood. That is why the location of your home is so important to its resale value. Also, properly maintaining your home will provide you with a sound place to live and also help your home to maintain its value.

Q. What factors determine how much of a home I can afford to purchase?

A. The amount of home you can afford depends upon a variety of factors, including your income, your debts, the amount of money you have for a down payment, the interest rate, and length of the mortgage. You should also consider ongoing expenses associated with the home, such as utilities, taxes, insurance, and maintenance, when determining how much of a home you are comfortable owning.

Housing Options

Q. We are relocating to an area we know nothing about. What should we look for when choosing a city or neighborhood?

A. Before purchasing a home in any area, thoroughly research all the options that are available. Where you live has a big impact on your quality of life. Decide what things are important to you. Are quality schools for the children the most important? Is a short commute to work on your list? Talk to people who live in the areas you are considering, check out the schools, and test-drive the commute. You should be sure before you buy. If you are still uncertain, consider renting for a while to give yourself more time to look around.

Q. **I keep hearing that location is one of the most important factors in choosing a home. Why?**

A. Here is why: Let's say you know exactly what you want in your home, and you have found two candidates. One is next to a busy, loud, major highway, and another is near a serene, babbling brook. Although the first home may have everything you want, it will probably never command the same price as the second home, and selling it will be more difficult. Location normally trumps every other consideration, both in terms of where to live and for resale value. The location of the home also plays a major role in determining the quality of life for its owners.

Q. **We are moving to a big city and are considering buying a co-op. What issues should we consider?**

A. As with any home purchase, you must thoroughly check things out before purchasing. A co-op is somewhat different than other housing options, so you need to look at a few items that are specific to co-ops as well. Be sure the co-op is financially stable and that management has plenty of money to run the building and pay for repairs and renovations. Talk to others to make sure management is reasonable and responsive. Get copies of the legal documents, including the bylaws, lease, and financial statements, and find out about the covenants, conditions, and restrictions (CC&Rs) so you can see if you agree to them. You may also want to consider hiring a lawyer who specializes in co-ops to review everything before you purchase.

Inspections

Q. **I have heard horror stories about homes with hazards such as lead, asbestos, and radon, and homes even being too close to high-voltage power lines. How can I avoid problems like this?**

A. Have the home thoroughly inspected for environmental hazards by a qualified inspector *before* you purchase. Living close to power lines has not conclusively been proven to be a hazard; however, you may consider them an eyesore and you may not want to live near them. Eyesores near a home can affect its resale value.

Q. **After we closed on our home, we found mold under the carpet. Can we sue anyone?**

A. Probably not. It is doubtful that the previous owner knew about the mold, since it was under the floor covering. Typically, inspectors do not check cosmetics like carpeting and paint. The inspector does not guarantee that the home won't have any problems; the inspector tells you what he or she finds. A hidden problem like this is probably beyond the scope of a regular inspection.

Q. **I am buying a home and found out that the roof leaks. Nowhere in any disclosure that I received from the seller did it mention roof problems. What do I do?**

A. Some states require sellers to disclose all known defects to the buyer as part of the escrow process. But even if you do not have such a law in your state, your agent should have made such disclosures a contingency of your offer. If the seller knew about the defect but didn't disclose it, he or she may have defrauded you, which could be a reason to pull out of the contract. A better course of action would be to have the seller agree to pay for the cost of fixing the problem. As opposed to getting stuck with the house, he or she might just agree to it. This problem also underscores the need for a thorough inspection before the closing.

Insurance

Q. **How much insurance coverage do I need?**

A. You should have adequate protection in the event of a loss. When looking at insurance coverage, focus on removing or reducing the financial risks associated with big calamities. Your insurance coverage should take care of big financial losses you can't handle on your own. Your insurance professional can help make sure you are adequately protected.

Q. **Do I need to purchase a homeowner's warranty in addition to homeowner's insurance?**

A. A homeowner's warranty is a type of insurance that will cover repairs to items such as heating and air-conditioning systems, the hot water heater, or appliances if they fail during the time period covered. Homeowner's insurance is an insurance policy that provides coverage for your property and personal liability needs. The buyer or the seller can pay for a homeowner's warranty, and it can help both parties. A homeowner's warranty provides protection for the buyer, should a covered item fail, and it may help the seller with the sale of the home by offering the buyer added value.

Mortgages

Q. We find the many mortgages and options confusing. Is there some simple way to sort them out?

A. When comparing mortgages, be sure to compare all the terms of each loan, including the length of the loan, interest rate, annual percentage rate (APR), number of points charged, closing costs, prepayment penalties, miscellaneous fees, down payment required, and so forth. You'll want to make sure you look at all of the terms of each mortgage to ensure you make an accurate comparison.

Q. What is a good faith estimate?

A. A good faith estimate is, as the name implies, an estimate of the loan fees you can expect to pay prior to closing, as well as your estimated closing and escrow costs. A lender must supply the good faith estimate within three days of your loan application.

Q. What is loan fraud and how do I avoid it?

A. Loan fraud occurs when you are induced to enter into a loan thinking it is one thing, but it turns out the loan is something altogether different. Buyers can end up paying above market interest rates and fees. Unscrupulous lenders sometimes rely on fine print to clear them of any responsibility for promises that were made to induce the borrower to sign. To avoid loan fraud, be sure you read and understand everything before you sign, never sign a blank document, and check out the lender thoroughly before doing business.

Q. My lender said something about a loan-to-value ratio on the home we are considering purchasing. What does that mean?

A. The loan-to-value ratio (referred to as LTV) is a percentage relationship between the amount of the loan and the appraised value or sales price (whichever is lower) of the home. The LTV helps determine how much down payment is required and the homebuyer's initial equity in the home. For example, if your loan has an LTV of 90 percent and the house is selling for $150,000, the loan could be for 90 percent of that, or $135,000. You would need to come up with a $15,000 down payment, which would represent your beginning equity in the home. A higher LTV for a particular loan would indicate that less money would be needed for a down payment. Conventional mortgages with LTVs greater than 80 percent also require private mortgage insurance.

Q. I am a veteran. Do I get any breaks when purchasing a home?

A. You may qualify for a low-cost loan if you were on active duty ninety consecutive days during wartime or one hundred eighty-one days during peacetime, or if you spent six years in the Reserves or National Guard. There is an additional often overlooked benefit: Unmarried surviving spouses of veterans who died on active duty or as the result of a service-connected disability are also eligible for VA home loans. Some veterans are entitled to borrow up to $240,000 with no down payment. Call your local VA office or log on to www.va.gov for more information.

Q. **I was laid off from my job six months ago, and I don't think I will be able to keep making my mortgage payments. What should I do?**

A. If necessary, consider borrowing the necessary money from a friend or family member to keep making your payments. Talk to your lender to determine your options. Lenders often have programs that allow you to wrap a delinquency into the end of the loan. As a last resort, Chapter 13 bankruptcy will allow you to stay in the home and catch up on the debts over a three- to five-year period.

Q. **Does my mother qualify for a reverse mortgage? She is sixty-five.**

A. Yes, she probably does. Generally, to qualify for a reverse mortgage, homeowners must be at least age sixty-two, occupy the home as a principal residence, and have no mortgage (or only one or two payments left). This type of mortgage enables senior citizens who need cash to borrow against the value of their homes. The loan can be paid out in a lump sum or monthly or can be set up as a line of credit and tapped as needed. The amount available depends on the age, value, and location of the home.

Your mother would need to continue to pay property taxes and insurance and make repairs to maintain the value of the property.

Offers

Q. **We are about to buy a new home. What is negotiable?**

A. *Everything* is negotiable! You can negotiate everything in the home buying process, including but not limited to the purchase price, the contract terms, what is included with the home, who will pay for what, and the date of the closing. Essentially, everything is negotiable. But remember, you should concentrate on those items that are important to you. Choose carefully which battles to fight to avoid spoiling the deal.

Q. **I am worried that my initial offer will be too high. What do I do?**

A. Your initial offer should depend on several factors: comparable home sales in the area, the condition of the house, how hot the market is, how much you can afford, how long the house has been for sale, how badly you want it, and the seller's need to sell. Remember that first offers are rarely accepted, so start out with a low (but reasonable) offer and see what happens. You will probably end up reaching a compromise somewhere between your offer and the seller's initial asking price.

Q. **What is an earnest money deposit and why do I have to pay it?**

A. An earnest money deposit is a deposit you make with your offer to show the seller that you are serious (earnest) about purchasing the home. If your offer is accepted, the earnest money is applied to your down payment. However, if your offer is accepted and then you decide you don't want the home, you will lose your earnest money deposit. If your offer is not accepted, then your earnest money deposit is returned to you.

Points

Q. **What are points?**

A. Points are a type of fee paid to your lender when you close on your mortgage. They are actually figured in percentages—one point is equal to 1 percent of the total loan amount. A one-point fee on a $100,000 mortgage is $1,000; 1.5 points will cost you $1,500. When comparing mortgage rates, say 6.45 percent and 7 percent, you need to know how many points both lenders are charging. The lower rate may not always be better if you have to pay more points.

Q. **Should I pay points?**

A. Many homebuyers want to avoid points, but that may not always be a good idea. Generally, the more points you pay, the lower the interest rate on your loan. A rule of thumb is to equate each point with −.25 percent interest rate. If you pay an extra point on a 7 percent mortgage, that should lower your interest rate to about 6.75 percent. Is it worth it? It depends on how long you expect to stay in the home. If you plan to stay many years, paying extra points up front might save you some money in the long run. If, on the other hand, you expect to move to another home in just a few years, you generally shouldn't pay extra points. Your lender can determine whether paying extra points up front would be worthwhile for you.

Q. **On the closing statement for my principal residence, some of my costs are identified as points. Are points currently deductible?**

A. If the points represent fees that you paid solely for the use of money, they may be deductible as qualified residence interest. A fee that you pay as a specific service charge in connection with a loan is a charge for services rendered and is not deductible as interest. Here are the current criteria for the points to be deductible in full for the year paid:

1. The underlying loan has to be for the purchase or improvement of, and secured by, your principal residence.
2. The charging of points must be an established business practice in your area, and the points you pay are not in excess of the usual amount charged in your area.

3. The amount is computed as a percentage of the stated principal amount of the mortgage.

4. You must pay at closing an amount at least equal to the points charged. Money for this payment must come from a source other than the lender.

5. The points must be clearly shown on the settlement statement.

Before you automatically deduct the points all at once, check with your tax professional to determine if electing to deduct the points over the life of the loan is a better option.

Remodeling

Q. **We would like to make some renovations to our home. What should we do?**

A. First, you need a plan. If you don't start the process knowing what the end result should be and how much it will cost, you may wind up with something entirely different at a huge cost. Consider hiring a remodeling professional who can work with you to help define your needs and come up with a plan. Once you have your plan in hand, you can pass it to a reputable contractor who can make it happen. You may be able to do the work yourself, but you should start the process with a careful plan.

Saving Money

Q. **Is it possible to pay off my mortgage early?**

A. It depends upon the terms of your mortgage. If your mortgage includes a prepayment penalty, paying it off early may not be in your best interest. If your mortgage has no such penalty, paying off the mortgage early may make sense. Whether it's making a few additional payments a year, paying an additional amount each month, or paying a lump sum amount, paying off a mortgage early can reduce both the length of the mortgage and the amount of interest paid. Be sure to inform the lender that the additional payment(s) is to be applied to the loan's principal.

Q. **We went with a fixed-rate mortgage because we wanted to be certain about the amount we would have to pay each month. Interest rates have dropped below our fixed rate. Is there anything we can do?**

A. Refinancing may make sense for you. To make this decision, you must determine if you can recoup the costs associated with obtaining the new mortgage. If you plan to live in your house for several years and can save at least 1–2 percent from your current rate, refinancing may be a smart move. But before refinancing, make sure that it is the right move for your personal financial situation.

Q. **How much do you save with a 15-year mortgage compared to a 30-year mortgage?**

A. Generally, a 15-year mortgage requires you to pay a little less than half the total interest cost of the traditional 30-year fixed-rate mortgage. You also own your home in half the time. Lenders usually offer a 15-year mortgage at a slightly lower interest rate than a 30-year mortgage. The disadvantage: Monthly payments are 10 to 15 percent higher than with a 30-year mortgage.

Taxes

Q. **When do I get all the great tax benefits from owning a home?**

A. Generally, certain expenses related to home ownership, such as points, mortgage loan interest, prepayment penalties, and real estate taxes, are deductible. When you pay interest on a qualified home mortgage, you may generally deduct the interest in full as an itemized deduction. Points are also usually deductible in full, if certain conditions are met, in the year paid or over the lifetime of the loan. In addition, you can also deduct state, local, and foreign real estate taxes you pay on your home.

Q. **My wife and I recently sold our principal home. How can we avoid paying a large amount in taxes?**

A. If:

- Either you or your wife lived in the home for at least two of the five years immediately preceding the sale;
- During that five-year period, either of you owned the home for at least two years;
- Neither of you have sold another home within the past two years; and
- You file jointly

you can exclude from tax (meaning you will pay no tax on) up to $500,000 of gain. The maximum exclusion amount is $250,000 for taxpayers not filing a joint return. You pay tax on any gain in excess of your maximum exclusion amount. If you were in the home less than two years, the taxable gain may or may not be prorated, depending on your circumstances.

Q. **I am a single woman and I want to buy my first home. Can I use my IRA?**

A. You can withdraw up to $10,000 from an IRA to finance a first-time home purchase without incurring the 10-percent penalty tax for early withdrawals. However, distribution of any pretax earnings from a traditional IRA will be taxed as ordinary income. You can take advantage of this tax break only if you had no ownership interest in a principal residence during the two-year period ending on the date on which you buy the new home. There are some other technical but equally important provisions concerning using IRA funds to purchase a first home, so check with your tax professional *before* you take any money from an IRA.

Q. **I am considering purchasing a home, but the property's tax information was not included in the listing information. How do I find out how much the taxes are?**

A. If you have been looking at other comparable homes in the area, check if any of them listed the property tax information. That should give you a reasonable estimate. If not, or if you want information on a specific home, contact the assessor's office to find out what the current assessed value is and what the tax rate is. You may also want to find out when the property is due for reassessment or if the tax levy is scheduled to change.

Now, Get Ready to Make the Most of Your Home Buying Experience

ongratulations! You've finished reading the *H&R Block Home Buying Advisor*. You should now know a great deal more about the home buying process. You can begin the journey toward realizing your own home ownership goals and dreams by taking the fundamentals covered in these pages and applying them to your personal situation.

Remember, you don't have to travel alone on your journey toward home ownership. You may want to or need to work with certain professionals on some of the more complicated issues or those you want someone else to handle for you. Don't forget about your online learning resource, hrblock.com/advisor, which gives you access to a variety of interactive tools and calculators to help you get started.

We hope this book has helped you learn how to map out a plan to make your home ownership goals a reality. As you travel toward your destination, there will certainly be navigational adjustments you will need to make. Regardless of the detours, remember to stay focused on your home ownership goals. With a well-conceived home buying plan, desire, and persistence, you can make it happen. Happy home buying!

resources

Appraisers

To find out more about real estate appraisers or to locate one near you, contact:

- American Society of Appraisers (ASA)
  www.appraisers.org

- Appraisal Institute
  www.appraisalinstitute.org

- National Association of Independent Fee Appraisers (NAIFA)
  www.naifa.com

- National Association of Master Appraisers (NAMA)
  www.masterappraisers.org

- National Association of Real Estate Appraisers (NAREA)
  www.iami.org/narea

Co-ops

For more information about housing cooperatives, including finding, buying, and living in a co-op, contact:

- National Association of Housing Cooperatives (NAHC)
  www.coophousing.org

Credit Counseling

For information about low-cost or no-cost organizations that may be able to help you rebuild your credit or get out of debt, contact:

- Federal Trade Commission (FTC)
  www.ftc.gov

- National Foundation for Credit Counseling (NFCC)
  www.nfcc.org

Credit Reports

To order a copy of your credit report, report fraud, or correct an error, contact one of the three credit reporting services:

- Equifax
  www.equifax.com or 800-685-1111

- Experian
  www.experian.com or 888-397-3742

- TransUnion
  www.transunion.com or 800-888-4213

Credit Scores

To find out how credit scoring works, what your score is, and tips on improving it, contact:

- myFico
  www.myfico.com

Homebuilders' Association

To find your local homebuilders' association and for more information about building, owning, and remodeling a home, contact:

- National Association of Home Builders
  www.nahb.org

Home Equity

To find out more about using the equity in your home for items like refinancing, home equity loans, or debt consolidation, contact:

- H&R Block
  www.hrblock.com or 877-HRBLOCK (877-472-5625)

Home Inspection

To learn more about home inspections and to locate an inspector near you, contact:

- **American Society of Home Inspectors (ASHI)**
  www.ashi.com

- **National Association of Home Inspectors, Inc. (NAHI)**
  www.nahi.org

Home Ownership

To obtain more information about buying and selling homes, the value of home ownership, how to select a mortgage lender, and various financing options, contact:

- **U.S. Department of Housing and Urban Development (HUD)**
  www.hud.gov or 800-669-9777

H&R Block can provide you with comprehensive information on home mortgages, including first-time home buying, refinancing, home equity loans, and debt consolidation. You can also find educational information and many useful tools and calculators to help you make informed home ownership-related decisions.

- **H&R Block**
  www.hrblock.com or 877-HRBLOCK (877-472-5625)

Housing Discrimination Complaints

To learn more about housing discrimination or to file a complaint, contact:

- **U.S. Department of Housing and Urban Development (HUD)**
  www.hud.gov or 800-669-9777

Insurance

To learn more about all types of insurance, including a variety of products and services, about how to compare policies, and about the companies that issue the policies, contact:

- **A.M. Best Company**
  www.ambest.com

- **Insurance Information Institute**
  www.iii.org

- **National Association of Insurance Commissioners**
  www.naic.org

Miscellaneous Consumer Information

Information on a variety of topics including home ownership, home safety, the environment, and money matters can be obtained from the federal government. Contact:

- **FirstGov**
  www.consumer.gov

Mortgages

To obtain more information on how to select a mortgage lender and find various financing options, contact:

- **Federal Home Loan Mortgage Corporation (Freddie Mac)**
  www.freddiemac.com

- **Federal National Mortgage Association (Fannie Mae)**
  www.fanniemae.com

- **Government National Mortgage Association (Ginnie Mae)**
  www.ginniemae.gov

- U.S. Department of Agriculture (USDA) Rural Housing Service
  www.rurdev.usda.gov/rhs

- U.S. Department of Veterans Affairs (VA)
  www.va.gov

H&R Block can provide you with comprehensive information on home mortgages, including first-time home buying, refinancing, home equity loans, and debt consolidation.

- H&R Block
  www.hrblock.com or 877-HRBLOCK (877-472-5625)

Personal Finance

H&R Block can provide you with a wide range of personal finance information. Understand the tax and financial aspects of major life events, use online resources and tools to see how fast your savings can grow, prepare your taxes online, get your tax questions answered, learn the basics of investing, get quotes, invest online, pre-qualify for a mortgage, plus much more.

- H&R Block
  www.hrblock.com or 800-HRBLOCK (800-472-5625)

Realtors®

To find out more about Realtors® or to find one in your area, contact:

- National Association of Realtors®
  www.realtor.com

Remodeling

To find out more information about remodeling and selecting a remodeling professional, contact:

- National Association of the Remodeling Industry (NARI)
  www.nari.org

Taxes

For a variety of resource material including forms, publications, advice, and tax-related tools, contact:

- Internal Revenue Service (IRS)
  www.irs.gov or 800-829-1040

H&R Block has a wide selection of available resources for you. These include tax preparation and filing options, forms, advice, planning tools, tax preparation courses, and much more. To find out more, visit the retail location nearest you or contact:

- H&R Block
  www.hrblock.com or 800-HRBLOCK (800-472-5625)

index

about H&R Block

H&R Block, Inc. (www.hrblock.com) is a diversified company with subsidiaries that deliver tax services and financial advice, investment and mortgage products and services, and business accounting and consulting services.

As the world's largest tax services company, H&R Block served nearly 21 million clients during fiscal year 2003. Clients were served at H&R Block's approximately 10,600 retail offices worldwide, with its award-winning software, Tax-Cut®, and through its online tax services.

Investment services and securities products are offered through H&R Block Financial Advisors, Inc., member NYSE, SIPC. H&R Block, Inc. and H&R Block Services, Inc. are not registered broker-dealers. H&R Block Mortgage Corp. offers retail mortgage products. Option One Mortgage Corp. offers wholesale mortgage products and a wide range of mortgage services. RSM McGladrey, Inc. serves midsized businesses with accounting, tax, and consulting services.

Call **H&R Block Mortgage** today to get a
free, no obligation
Custom Mortgage Analysis.

At H&R Block Mortgage, our goal is to make sure you find the loan or refinance option that's appropriate for your specific needs. We have a variety of loan products, so you may qualify to:

- Refinance your mortgage and lower your monthly payments
- Consolidate other debts into one simple loan payment
- Make home improvements
- Borrow money for college tuition
- Get cash out

Call now at **1-877-HRBLOCK**
It just takes a few minutes.

H&R BLOCK
mortgage

EQUAL HOUSING
LENDER

Get a **free** financial review
and a **good night's sleep**.

Whether you're saving for a new home, higher education, or a much-needed vacation, our experienced financial advisors will help you plan your financial future so you can rest easy.

To schedule your appointment at an H&R Block office near you, call 1-800-HRBLOCK (select the Financial and Investment Services option) today.

Call **1-800-HRBLOCK** today and get a free Financial Review.

H&R BLOCK®
financial advisors

WE HELPED PEOPLE WHO OVERPAID GET BACK AN AVERAGE OF $1,300.

CAN YOU SAY "CHA-CHING"

Take the FREE Double Check Challenge at H&R Block

Thousands of Americans overpaid nearly $1 billion in taxes last year. Did you overpay? H&R Block will double check your past years' returns to see if you're entitled to more money back.

Those who overpaid and refiled with us got an average of $1,300 back. Have us double-check your previous years' tax returns free to see if we can find you more. And, we can help you re-file* past returns so you can get back the money you deserve.

See reverse side for more details.

H&R BLOCK

just plain smart™

find money

you didn't even know you'd lost.

Double Check Challenge

Americans overpay nearly $1 billion in taxes each year.
Is some of it yours?

How it Works

1. Bring copies of your past returns to an H&R Block office.

2. Our H&R Block professionals will review up to three years of past returns - at no cost to you.

3. If we discover an error, we can help you re-file past returns so you can get back the money you deserve (re-filing fees apply).

Benefits

Found money - Clients who overpaid and re-filed with us received an average of $1,300 back.

Join the long list of clients who took - and benefited - from the Double Check Challenge

H&R BLOCK®